Consumer Management in the Internet Age

Consumer Management in the Internet Age

How Customers Became Managers in the Modern Workplace

Joshua Sperber

LEXINGTON BOOKS
Lanham • Boulder • New York • London

Published by Lexington Books
An imprint of The Rowman & Littlefield Publishing Group, Inc.
4501 Forbes Boulevard, Suite 200, Lanham, Maryland 20706
www.rowman.com

6 Tinworth Street, London SE11 5AL

British Library Cataloguing in Publication Information Available

Library of Congress Cataloging-in-Publication Data

Names: Sperber, Joshua, author.
Title: Consumer management in the Internet age : how customers became managers in the modern workplace / Joshua Sperber.
Description: Lanham : Lexington Books, [2019] | Includes bibliographical references and index.
Identifiers: LCCN 2018057741 (print) | LCCN 2019000433 (ebook) | ISBN 9781498592222 (Electronic) | ISBN 9781498592215 (cloth : alk. paper) | ISBN 9781498592239 (pbk: alk. paper)
Subjects: LCSH: Electronic commerce. | Internet marketing. | Consumers. | Customer relations. | Customer services.
Classification: LCC HF5548.32 (ebook) | LCC HF5548.32 .S649 2019 (print) | DDC 658.8/72--dc23
LC record available at https://lccn.loc.gov/2018057741

™ The paper used in this publication meets the minimum requirements of American National Standard for Information Sciences Permanence of Paper for Printed Library Materials, ANSI/NISO Z39.48-1992.

Printed in the United States of America

Table of Contents

Acknowledgments

This work began as a dissertation at the City University of New York Graduate Center, where I was tremendously fortunate to have Frances Fox Piven, Corey Robin, and Joe Rollins on my committee. They expertly and generously guided this project from its inception.

Khalilah Walters, Elliot Sperber, E.J. Hamacher, and Kristofer Petersen-Overton provided exceptionally helpful advice for improving the work. My grasp of the subject was additionally strengthened through a series of broader conversations I had with Geoffrey McDonald, Malcolm Dunn, Joel White, and Heather Klingelsmith.

I also received much helpful feedback and support from people I met at or through the Grad Center including Sobukwe Odinga, Aaron Shapiro, Joanna Tice Jen, Alan Koenig, Puangchon Unchanam, Amy Schiller, Lizzie Eisenberg, Douglas Medina, Wilson Sherwin, Luke Elliott-Negri, Jeffrey Broxmeyer, Adam McMahon, Mike Miller, John McMahon, Asaf Shamis, Robert Castle, Liz Nelson, Fanny Lauby, Chris McKinley, Lucia Green-Weiskel, Yekaterina Oziashvili, Chris Michael, Gerry Martini, Andre Guzzi, Guy Feldman, Neil Hernandez, Erika Iverson, Dan Rogers, Humayun Kabir, Tom Waters, Kamran Moshref, Ximena Garcia Bustamante, Emily Crandall, Rachel Brown, Jon Keller, Jorge Matos, and Kabir Dandona.

I am indebted to several anonymous reviewers whose perspicacious readings of the manuscript and supportive advice dramatically improved it.

I feel very fortunate to have worked with Nicolette Amstutz, Jessica Tepper, and Megan Murray at Lexington Books, all of whom demonstrated great consideration, patience, and thoughtfulness in bringing the project to light.

New Labor Forum and *Counterpunch* provided me platforms to develop and share ideas that are in this book.

This work is in part the culmination of many years of learning under the tutelage of outstanding teachers. Ironically, four of the finest teachers I've ever had—Nicholas De Genova, Thaddeus Russell, Christopher R. Jackson, and Deborah A. Gerson—were not retained at the universities where I learned from them, illustrating that exemplary teaching often occurs not because of but in spite of the university. I dedicate this to them and to all other teachers who have undeservedly been separated from their students and their craft.

Introduction

In the mid-1990s I worked for three restaurants. Although one, Coco's Bakery Restaurant, was part of a large national conglomerate and two were family-owned and run, all three regularly emphasized the importance of my being friendly and accommodating to customers. Whereas I was lectured by my bosses at all three restaurants about my needing to smile more, at Coco's my expressions of warmth (as well as my other duties) were not only monitored by managers but also by company mystery shoppers who posed as customers in order to periodically observe and report on our restaurant's performance. Our managers regularly warned me that because we could never know who might be a mystery shopper it was imperative to please every customer, and I was in fact reprimanded after my failure to smile at a mystery shopper hurt one of our evaluations.

Two things struck me about the ways in which managers discussed these mystery shoppers. The first was that managers referred to them as if they were autonomous customers rather than who they actually were: company employees whose job was to spy on us. It often crossed my mind to suggest to my managers that we ought to just tell the corporate office to order the mystery shoppers to relax their standards and then nobody would get written up and everyone could be happy. Of course, this unspoken suggestion was designed to acknowledge and play with the disingenuousness of management's invocation of mystery shoppers as an authority external to the restaurant itself. It was quite clear to me that the mystery shoppers were another arm of management, albeit one that could penetrate where managers could not by more intimately observing employees' physical and emotional labor. Even though I lived at home at the time and also assumed that I could obtain other work if I were fired, my awareness of the existence of these mystery shoppers altered the way I thought about—and on some level acted toward—customers.

The second thing that struck me about this experience was the transparent selectiveness with which managers addressed customers' concerns. I had seen managers refuse all manner of customer requests, as unsatisfied customers attempted to have their bills reduced, the music turned down, or their entrees altered to no avail. It was sometimes hard to believe that these dissatisfied customers were the same people who are, as the maxim declares, "always right." It was exceedingly clear that, in the eyes of management, they were not. Indeed, the very notion of consumer infallibility is negated by the more prosaic but no less ubiquitous assertion that "management reserves the right to refuse service to anyone"—that is, to determine who gets to be a customer in the first place. After all, there are customers who, justly or not, have been banned from restaurants, bars, and all manner of other establishments. It seemed then that managers who gave me grief about my disinclination to "seem happy" were not merely concerned about pleasing the customer, at least not in a universal sense (many customers were oblivious to us and some were clearly turned off by the aggressively saccharine attitudes a few of our colleagues displayed). We were to please the customer but only insofar as and in the manner that our managers said; that is, it was not the customer but the manager who was "always right."

It was with this experience in mind that I began to think about the website Yelp. I have often thought about the ways in which, if I worked in a restaurant today, I would be affected by what seemed to me to be that website's millions of unpaid mystery shoppers. I suspected that restaurant managers used Yelp reviews as a form of free customer surveillance and invoked them to discipline employees, and I wanted to find out if this were true. And, if so, I wanted to look at the ways in which Yelp reviews change how restaurant employees think about and perform their work. Finally, I wanted to investigate the reviewers' role in this dynamic. Specifically, why do reviewers take time out of their days to write frequently long and detailed online reviews for which they are not paid? Do they write reviews for fun, for revenge, for a sense of social duty? Is the frequent assumption among both social scientists and laypeople that reviewers are primarily inspired by either strongly positive or strongly negative motivations accurate?

As I thought more about Yelp I began to notice how online consumer reviews might affect other occupations. One of these occupations was, in fact, right under my nose, as I had worked as an adjunct professor, on and off, from 2013–2018 and have been subject to not only department-provided student evaluations but also student reviews on the Rate My Professors (RMP) website, which I, like most adjuncts, kept close tabs on. At the beginning of the spring semester of 2018, which began after I completed the bulk of my research on RMP, I was notified by the community college where I was teaching that nine sections in our department had been canceled because they had failed to meet the minimum enrollment requirement of fifteen students. If the school fails to cancel an underenrolled course it can be fined by the state, yet in the past the school often refused to cancel these courses and accepted the fines. Due to a number of factors—including long-term budgetary restrictions—the school is presently unwilling to accept these fines and has thereby followed state requirements to slash the classes.

I was admittedly relieved that none of my three courses was canceled, although I was overwhelmed on the first day of class when approximately sixty students, many of them standing along the walls or sitting on the floor, squeezed into each of my first two classes. Notably, these courses are designed for a maximum of forty-five students, but we had been instructed by the department chair to turn no one away. My overloaded sections should not have come as a surprise given the cancellation of other sections. After all, the students who were enrolled in those canceled sections needed somewhere else to go. While I knew that there were a variety of reasons for underenrollment (e.g., the expansion of online courses has particularly hurt enrollment in night classes, since students understandably prefer to be home at the end of the day), I wondered what role, if any, RMP played in underenrolling some classes and overenrolling others. I then had six RMP ratings for this school, and they were uniformly "positive." I am using scare quotes insofar as positive ratings on RMP do not necessarily correspond to pedagogical efficacy. On the contrary, after awarding me with a perfect rating of five, one of my reviewers, to my chagrin, advised fellow students to take my courses in part because I am an "#easyA." Irrespective of my actual rigor (I in fact fail students every semester), I am clearly perceived as an easy grader. I wondered about the RMP ratings of those adjuncts who had lost their sections (one of these adjuncts, who had lost two classes, is convinced that her paucity of RMP reviews harmed her enrollment numbers). While it is challenging to conduct a comparison between enrollments in identical courses taught by different instructors at the same time (i.e., to isolate the arguable role of RMP), the very fact that some of us were thinking about the influence of RMP on course cancellations is indicative of the way in which RMP has gotten into some of our heads. Indeed, RMP—specifically my *awareness* of my reviews—has influenced my teaching. I recall once being pleased, and somewhat surprised, to read that a reviewer described me as "caring." Knowing that this description was now part of my public teaching reputation, I became more conscious of it and have alternately embraced it and, lest I coddle students too much, bridled against it. In either case, it has affected me in a way that department-issued, private, student evaluations have not.

Precisely because restaurants are so different from colleges and universities, I thought that it would be instructive to compare and contrast the ways in which online customer reviews on Yelp and RMP respectively affect each. While restaurants are a quintessential component of the service sector, colleges and universities retain traces, at least in their self-conceptions, of their medieval origins based on duty and mutual obligation. And while restaurant workers are partially beholden to customers whose tips constitute the bulk of servers' wages, instructors are solely paid by their employers and, by contrast, do not serve students so much as teach and evaluate them, often to the latter's dismay. Thus, the economic mechanisms and normative practices governing instructors and servers are quite different, as are the expectations placed on students and diners.

Yet, notwithstanding these and other differences, Yelp reviews and RMP reviews, as I show in chapters 3 and 4, influence restaurants and colleges and universities in similar ways in their ultimate effects on workers and should be thought of as what Fuller and Smith have called "customer management" (Fuller and Smith 1991), a practice that has existed since the advent of the first department stores in the late nineteenth century but has quantitatively and qualitatively expanded through the Internet. Specifically, both websites help discipline workers and in so doing alter workers' thoughts and work habits.

Regardless of whether consumer managers post reviews to criticize, compliment, or merely dispassionately describe workers, such activity should be seen as a form of highly contingent and politically conservative power. It is my emphasis on the conservative—specifically, antilabor—effects of consumer management that helps distinguish this study from numerous other accounts of consumer society. While such accounts often view consumers as either progressive political actors or apolitical dupes (or even paradoxically, a la Slavoj Žižek [Žižek 2009], self-aware dupes), this book focuses on a particular form of consumer activity that expresses both relative consumer agency and antilabor conservatism, regardless of whether reviewers are motivated by notions of consumer solidarity or merely consider online reviewing to be an enjoyable hobby. Indeed, partly due to its casual and recreational character, online consumer management does not initially appear to be a political activity at all. Yet, I argue, it is profoundly shaped by the ideological presuppositions and material demands of twenty-first-century capitalism and in that regard can tell us much about the character, and constraints, of contemporary life.

SEVERAL NOTES ON METHODS

Whereas there are numerous consumer-based rating sites, I focus on Yelp and RMP for several reasons. Yelp and RMP are two of the most popular sites not only in their respective industries but in general. As such, they have greater social, cultural, and economic influence than do smaller sites and, as I argue below, are particularly emblematic of a significant transformation in the evolution of contemporary capitalism. On a more practical note, it is likelier that more readers will have had experiences with these sites as opposed to smaller, and relatively newer, sites. Moreover, websites, as with all businesses, frequently come and go. While there can be great value in examining businesses that fail, focusing on ones that have already established relative longevity increases the chances that my analysis, at least in this respect, will retain more immediate relevance over time. Furthermore, my case studies were selected not only because of the size and prominence of the two websites but also because of the specific industries they concern: education and restaurants, industries selected due to my personal experience with them as well as my contention that they ideally present similarities and differences that are highly conducive to a comparative analysis.

Rather than being seen as statistically representative, the research described below reflects my efforts to present a series of illustrative cases whose relative lack of breadth enabled me to analyze their themes in greater depth. It is fair to ask, as some have done, how data that are not necessarily statistically representative can have general relevance. In response, we can, by way of example, look at the U.S. prison system, which holds approximately two million prisoners. Although this is a massive number of human beings in absolute terms, it reflects less than 1 percent of the total population of the country. Further, there is an even smaller number of prisoners who are held in solitary confinement, prisons within prisons. The number of these prisoners represents but a miniscule fraction of the total U.S. population. Nevertheless, such populations, even if they are not statistically representative of the larger society, warrant study. The very extremity of such cases—for instance, their brutality and cruelty—can in fact tell us something about the institutional logic, values, and sensibilities of the larger society. Whereas the prison system is not the subject of this study, it is nonetheless true that through examining and extrapolating from the particular we can often learn much about the general.

Accordingly, my case studies on Yelp and RMP were primarily conducted using qualitative methods. I relied on dozens of formal and informal conversations with servers, bartenders, and fellow instructors (both adjuncts and full-time) as well as on surveys of and interviews with six sets of people: Yelp reviewers, restaurant and bar managers, restaurant and bar employees, RMP reviewers, department chairs, and college and university instructors, almost all of whom are adjuncts. My interviews with restaurant managers and servers were conducted primarily in New York City, and, while I generated research on the use of Yelp in a variety of restaurants, from large chains to mom and pops, my findings are still not statistically representative of the substantial variation among different business models not only in New York

City but also throughout the country. Such variation is significant, for instance, insofar as large and chain restaurants are relatively insulated from the effects of Yelp reviews, while small restaurants are highly vulnerable to them (Luca 2011). As my findings suggest, managers at smaller restaurants are, perhaps predictably, more ambivalent about and often openly hostile toward Yelp than are managers and spokespeople at large restaurants and chains. Similarly, while I sent over four hundred survey requests to chairs primarily in ten departments at public universities, liberal arts colleges, private universities, and community colleges throughout the United States, I aimed to attract a broad, rather than statistically representative per se, range of responses. Again, the lack of statistical representativeness is significant as department chairs at different universities and colleges appear to have different attitudes toward and relationships with RMP. In general, department chairs at public universities and liberal arts colleges either assert that they do not consult RMP or are openly hostile to it. By contrast, several department chairs at community colleges acknowledged reading and relying on the site.

Beyond conducting in-person interviews in restaurants and bars and soliciting surveys via email, I solicited surveys via instant messaging through my Yelp account. I additionally joined several dozen Facebook college and university groups, adjunct groups, and restaurant groups in order to solicit instructors, RMP reviewers, servers, and restaurant managers to complete surveys. Finally, I solicited surveys from servers through publishing a guest post on a server-themed blog. A small number of surveys were completed over email, but the vast majority were completed through the website Survey Monkey. Although I joined a diverse set of Facebook groups, I need to account for respondents' selection bias insofar as those with strong views on RMP or Yelp were quite possibly likelier to respond to my posted invitations. Indeed, several restaurant managers enthusiastically agreed to be interviewed since, as they told me, they hate Yelp. Further, I did not randomly send survey requests on the Yelp website, but instead, following the format of the website, used snowball sampling, surveying friends of friends who appeared on a given page. Additionally, I specifically sought to survey "Elite" Yelp reviewers since these users generate a disproportionate number of reviews on the site. My use of quantitative methods consisted of several survey questions based on numerical ratings and word counts of my survey responses and online reviews. For example, it was through such word counts that I discovered that there is a high percentage of reviewers who are motivated to "help" others, and, following the work of Ben Schmidt (2015), that RMP reviews deploy consistently sexist language.

Finally, I address my own experiences as an adjunct professor and a (pre-Yelp) restaurant worker, which brings up the issue of bias. My epistemological point of departure is that bias is unavoidable. In contrast to positivist assumptions of an objective world that can be scrutinized by a detached outside observer, we—not least in our inherited languages and the concepts they articulate—are ultimately part and parcel of the very things we wish to examine (Burawoy 1991; 2009). There was, for instance, inevitable bias in my decision to develop this project, as I considered it both interesting and important. Yet, insofar as my personal experiences have helped direct my research, I have attempted to restrict my values to the questions that I have asked irrespective of the, sometimes surprising, answers that they have produced. In sharing my own experiences and views, I have sought both to elaborate my account and to be explicit about my role within it. Whether this bias has diminished my interpretation of that account will be determined by the reader.

Chapter One

We're All Managers Now (and We're Doing It for Free)

Online consumer management,[1] the primary subject of this book, combines two discrete but overlapping phenomena: what has been referred to as prosumption and consumer management. An examination of online consumer management therefore requires understanding each of these two practices and the historical circumstances in which they converged. The neologism prosumption—a form of consumption in which consumers, or prosumers, are incorporated into the production process—was coined by Alvin Toffler in 1980 but describes a process that has been present in various forms throughout human history (Toffler 1980; Ritzer and Jurgenson 2010). As Marx and others have noted, consumption has always involved production (e.g., the act of eating reproduces one's body) just as production has always entailed consumption (e.g., the act of procreation consumes human energy) (Marx 1993 [1939], 90–94).

That production and consumption are interwoven certainly does not suggest that consumers and workers have somehow melded into a single entity. It is as true today as it was in the middle of the nineteenth century that consumers and workers occupy discrete roles within capitalism. Through purchasing goods, consumers help capitalists to realize profit, but the source of profit, Marx and those who have followed him have stressed, is in the surplus value that capitalists extract through their exploitation of waged labor.

Confronted with downward pressure on profit—for instance through an increase in competition or supply—capitalists have historically turned to a predictable toolkit to maintain growth, or at least ward off bankruptcy, that includes raising productivity (for instance, through the introduction of new technologies), eliminating workers, or merely reducing workers' wages. That is, capitalists, who are generally unable to reduce fixed expenses such as rent and equipment, have tended to apply cost-cutting, directly or indirectly, to labor.

The vulnerability of labor nevertheless does not suggest that consumers are accorded a privileged position within the system. Marx showed that capitalism is unique since it, as opposed to all other economic systems, is based on the production of items not for use value (with a logical endpoint once consumers' needs are met) but for exchange value (with no endpoint at all) (Marx 1992 [1867], chapter 4). The needs of consumers are thereby a subordinated means to the ends of capitalists' pursuit of the never-ending accumulation of capital; insofar as people's needs are met, it is incidental to a system of production that is based not on fulfilling people's needs per se but on capturing consumers' money to fuel further production. That is, capitalism is the only economic system in which consumers serve the needs of production rather than one in which production serves the needs of consumers.

The market, insofar as it is free from price fixing and other oligopolistic practices, generally discourages businesses from raising prices on customers, who are of course free to buy cheaper goods from rival businesses. However, there are other, subtler, ways in which consumers can be used to increase revenue or diminish costs for business. Beyond tactics such as planned obsolescence is the stratagem of incorporating consumers into the production process itself.

The demands that capitalism places on consumers are hardly limited to the ever-increasing consumption of commodities but include the various unpaid duties and activities of daily life that are required to sustain capitalism's social and economic infrastructures. Thus, prosumption has included everything from housework to selecting and bagging one's groceries to filling one's gas tank to navigating automated telephone directories to maintaining one's credit ratings, and could therefore be likened to the concept of "social reproduction" or Ivan Illich's description of the unpaid "shadow work" that, Illich emphasizes, "feeds the formal economy . . . (rather than) social subsistence" (Illich 1981, 8). With the emergence of the Internet, prosumption has expanded to encompass online intellectual production including everything from blog entries to comments on newspaper articles to homemade videos to the design of new products such as potato chips (Zwick, Bonsu, and Darmody 2008). Specifically, the Internet provided what earlier media, including radio and TV, could not, an interactive "mechanism of reply" that has enabled users to more intimately and comprehensively generate and contribute intellectual content to countless businesses (Adorno and Horkheimer 2002 [1944], 96; Zwick, Bonsu, and Darmody 2008).

Whereas prior to the Internet much of prosumption consisted of necessary, routinized, and often isolated tasks, consumer management from its inception has been largely voluntary, proactive, and by definition interactive. Customer management consists of the solicited or unsolicited unpaid monitoring of, directing of, and reporting on service workers by customers (Edwards 1984; Fuller and Smith 1991), a practice that has operated in workplaces from early twentieth century department stores to, on a far larger scale, the restaurants, bars, hospitals, ride-hail cars, and college classrooms of today (Hochschild 2003 [1983]; Benson 1988; Fuller and Smith 1991; Leidner 1993).

With the dramatic growth of the service sector since the 1970s, managers have increasingly confronted a dilemma in their desire to control workers who directly interact with customers: although it is undesirable to grant free reign to workers who interact with customers, too much control can stifle the spontaneity, creativity, and emotional receptivity that frequently define successful customer service (Fuller and Smith 1991; Hochschild 2003 [1983]). Business has in many cases attempted to resolve this dilemma, one that was exacerbated by new pressures on profit following the 1973 global downturn, by recruiting customers to manage workers. As with prosumption in general, customer management has exponentially increased with the advent of the Internet, which provides the technological capacity—"eyes that must see without being seen"—for the "hierarchical observation" that, along with "normalizing judgment," is a cornerstone of modern society (Foucault 1995 [1975], 170–71). As opposed to other forms of prosumption, however, online consumer management functions in two separate ways: it not only creates free content for websites but it also intensifies control over workers.

Online consumer management, then, can be defined as a practice in which customers monitor, report on, and discipline workers through writing and posting online reviews. Numerous consumer managers function in effect as informal "mystery shoppers," providing employers with an unpaid resource that they can call upon in their management of employees. Whereas consumer reviewers have a variety of motivations, the efficacy of their reviews is, depending on the industry, frequently contingent upon the needs of employers who invoke reviews in highly selective manners. While consumer reviewers frequently derive enjoyment and satisfaction from writing reviews and interacting within like-minded online communities, a paradoxical yet core contention of this book is that online consumer management is based on both exploitation and alienation.

EXPLOITATION AND ALIENATION: THE NEW NATIONAL PASTIMES?

Though counterintuitive, there need not be any contradiction in the idea that online consumer management can be satisfying and enjoyable and, at the same time, exploitative and alienating. Web 2.0 users in general provide website owners with, but are with rare exceptions excluded from,[2] virtually incalculable wealth. For instance, users contribute the unpaid content that helps draw visitors to Web 2.0 platforms in the first place, and this increased traffic is in turn leveraged to generate higher advertising revenue for site owners. Users also provide websites with monetizable personal data that are systematically collected, analyzed, and sold to outside buyers, a key characteristic of what Nick Srnicek has labeled "platform capitalism" (Srnicek 2017).

Notably, this generation of revenue occurs regardless of how much users enjoy and identify with their work. Whereas exploitation, as noted, refers to the extraction of surplus value from wage labor (slaves, therefore, are unable to produce surplus value insofar as they are not invested with a wage), we can describe users as exploited insofar as we recognize that the value they produce is nevertheless based on an ongoing, or "living," *exchange* with website (i.e., property) owners in which users are continually rewarded for their creation of online content with nonmonetary, psychological, rewards. On one hand, without the unpaid contributions of millions of users—performing what we might call *virtual* living labor—massive companies such as Facebook, Instagram, Yelp, and RMP would not be able to stay in business. On the other hand, whereas contributors do not receive a share in such companies' financial earnings, they are paid in kind through access to gratifying forms of communal activity and at times (consumer) solidarity—minus a *virtual* surplus that both adds monetary value to websites and, critically, keeps reviewers, who are never content with their earnings insofar as alienation is continually reproduced within a political economy predicated on private property, coming back for more. Nevertheless, if we adhere to Marx's conception of profit, we must still note that such activity, while producing astronomical wealth for platform owners, is unable to generate the *actual* surplus value that is the basis of economic growth in general—with one exception. Insofar as online consumer managers contribute to the intensification of the productivity of *wage laborers* (e.g., restaurant servers), we can identify an instance in which activity on Web 2.0 generates both wealth for individual firms *and* economic growth. That is, activities such as online consumer management, if practiced on a systematic and large enough scale, can potentially help steer capitalism away from its enduring crisis in profitability. However, in order to do so it must—as with other major historic technological-social transformations—restructure social norms and ultimately individuals themselves.

Consumer management additionally intensifies alienation, and it is here important to note that I am referring to alienation in two different respects. The first refers to a general sociological alienation, or ennui, involving a feeling of separation from the surrounding society. The second refers to workers' material alienation from the means of production that is a hallmark of capitalism. These two definitions are linked, and, historically, the second has helped reproduce the first (Marx 1994 [1844]). However, consumer management, which is voluntary and frequently personally rewarding, has arguably helped diminish the first form of alienation. As we will see, reviewers' descriptions of their involvement in a "community" defined by mutual duty and a shared "code" suggests that some of users' social needs are, at least in part, being met online. Crucially, however, this diminishment is accomplished through the intensification of the second form of alienation, as consumer managers do not own the websites on which they post reviews, notwithstanding their psychological investments in and identification with these sites. Reviewers encounter predesigned websites with formats that prompt them where and to varying degrees how to write their reviews. Websites are at times even redesigned, often disorienting users who then have to relearn how to navigate sites that, notwithstanding their personal commitments to them, are clearly not their own.[3] Consumer management's reproduction of the second form of alienation in fact suggests the tenuousness of consumer management's reduction of the first form of alienation. For example, as discussed in chapter 3, the carrots Yelp provides users through awarding "Elite" status can become sticks, as Yelp can withdraw "Elite" status from users if their productivity declines. That is, consumer management's diminishment of sociological alienation is problematic insofar as it is based on both the introduction of a new and precarious dependence on a given, privately owned, site and, in a larger sense, the reproduction of the system of capitalism in general. Because consumer management's reduction of the first form of alienation is not based on any larger material change in societal power relations, a mere website crash or closure can destroy an entire community. Consumer management does not address the structural sources of alienation and in fact reproduces them.

Additionally, Yelp and RMP provide forums that are not merely based on enjoyable social interaction but are also ideological in that they are characterized by consistent expressions of consumerist moral opposition to perceived wrongdoing, whether in the form of dishonest or inefficient business practices, incompetent or rude workers, or unfair or overly demanding instructors. The shared interests and purposes that unite online consumer managers and turn them into communities are therefore based on an intrinsically antagonistic relationship with other sectors of society. Later in this book I show that this antagonism most directly affects wage workers, who are surveilled and reported on either to managers who can punish servers or to other students who can affect adjuncts' professional prospects through altering course sizes. While I have not encountered any cases in which employers directly financially profit from consumer management (for instance, by reducing their reliance on formal paid management), consumer managers do increase disciplinary scrutiny and intensify the work of some employees who report working harder due to their awareness of online reviews. Although negative Yelp reviews can adversely affect small restaurants, Yelp more immediately and intimately affects restaurant workers, who are personally and at times cruelly criticized on that site, for which they are frequently disciplined and periodically fired. As a result, even workers who have never been subject to a Yelp review have changed their work habits due to their awareness of the possibility of being criticized on Yelp. Simultaneously, adjuncts have reported grading and returning papers faster and being more punctual, and in some cases grading more generously, due to their concerns over receiving negative RMP reviews. That is, the exploitation and alienation associated with online consumer management affect not only online reviewers but also the most vulnerable targets of reviews: workers.

CONSUMPTION FOR WHOM?

A rich, if tragic, irony of online consumer management is that although it is time consuming it does little to improve consumers' ultimate material well-being. This, however, should be unsurprising if we consider another central theme of this book: the consumer under capitalism is structurally weak. In fact, as discussed in chapter 2, modern consumers, who had been created only after seismic historical transformations in which masses of people were forced from the land and their means of subsistence, were in effect invented in order to absorb the glut produced by nineteenth century industrial manufacturing. While consumption would become more sophisticated over time, we should remember that consumers were initially taught—for instance, through the strategic use of trademarks, branding, packaging, and ubiquitous advertising informed by ever more sophisticated market research—not only to buy unprecedentedly large amounts of newly mass produced items but also new ways to buy or "shop" for them, an activity dependent on, for most, income earned from wage labor. Consumers are furthermore restricted not only by their income but also by the range of commodities that capitalists elect to produce in the first place, decisions that are not based on addressing social need but on maximizing profit. Consumers in this regard constitute a dependent rather than an independent variable. To be sure, consumers undoubtedly question the demands and offerings of capitalists, and they have helped upend innumerable entrepreneurial dreams through rejecting countless new products and businesses. Yet, while consumers surely affect individual capitalists, consumers, as a constitutive and subordinate element of capitalism, lack immediate and practical leverage over capitalism *as a system*. They can choose—at least in most cases—who to buy *from* but not the fact that they, outside of mass political resistance and organization, have to buy.

It is particularly notable that the demands placed on and benefits conferred to consumers have never been distributed evenly. Within the context of U.S. history, the market has particularly discriminated against people of color and women. Although a great deal has changed in our world during the past century, the specifically racialized and gendered formation of consumption in the contemporary United States should not be thought of as a relic of some bygone era but rather as a defining element of what capitalist consumption has always entailed: the regulation of social and economic stratifications of a class-based society. Today people of color, particularly African Americans, are routinely discriminated against in, among other areas, the financial and real estate markets and are commonly harassed while perusing upper-crust stores. For their part, women experience discrimination today in everything from the world of online gaming to the automobile industry. And, of course, the advertising industry has made an unimaginable fortune through using—constructing, we might say—images of female sexuality to sell a limitless array of products and services, objectifying women and girls in an already violent and misogynistic popular imagination.

Racism and sexism also, unsurprisingly, influence online consumer management. Yelp reviewers have been shown to discriminate against African American neighborhoods and have engaged in racist and sexist harassment of businesses and workers (Zukin, Lindeman, and Hurson 2015; Rajaee 2017; Goldberg 2014). RMP, both informally and formally via its chili pepper (which RMP has thankfully promised to discontinue as of 2018), encourages reviewers to sexually objectify instructors, which disproportionately harms women who are far likelier to struggle with being "taken seriously" in U.S. society, even by their own students. RMP reviewers additionally penalize instructors who have accents, disproportionately affecting non-white teachers from around the world (Subtirelu 2015; Jaschik 2015).

The continuing existence of racism and sexism on these sites hardly suggests that such practices are indelible fixtures of humanity, but instead indicates some of the ways in which racism, sexism, and other discriminatory practices attain a logical function, if not inevitability, within the context of an intrinsically competitive economic system in general and rating systems in particular. It is reasonable to surmise that even if racism and sexism were magically extricated from present-day society, new and arbitrary social antagonisms would almost assuredly appear in their place, providing convenient explanations for the identity of the system's "losers" rather than questioning the legitimacy of a system that necessitates the production of "losers" in the first place.

A NEW MANAGER FOR AN OLD ECONOMY?

My intention in examining the significance of online reviewer subcultures on Yelp and RMP is not merely to draw attention to a popular hobby practiced by at times eccentric and self-involved individuals. Rather, in describing online consumer management I am seeking to indicate some of the ways in which capitalism is evolving, and what this implies for the way we live and think about our lives. Of course, few of us are regular Yelp or RMP reviewers, and even fewer of us are those extreme reviewers who have created amateur careers out of writing hundreds and even thousands of reviews not only of restaurants but of seemingly every commercial activity under the sun. There are just not that many people who have the time, inclination, dedication, and even obsessiveness to go through the trouble of writing and posting their thoughts on their innumerable market transactions. Yet, I believe that we should pay attention to these online reviewers not necessarily because they are like us but because they show us where we all very well might be going. These online reviewers can be thought of as a consumer vanguard precociously adapting to the changing material and ideological demands that the digital economy is increasingly placing on all of us. It makes no difference if we, unlike many Yelp and RMP reviewers, lack the energy or desire to regularly go out of our way to rate the various workers who we have interactions with; business is increasingly bringing rating systems *to us*, and in some cases it is virtually compelling us to rate workers whether we want to or not.

Whether dealing with cable providers, drivers, teachers, servers, bartenders, cell phone companies, apartment management companies, or even doctors and dentists, more and more people are being prompted to rate workers who they have had transactions with. Requesting that customers rate employees is not new in itself. But what is new is the conspicuousness, insistence, and frequency with which companies make these requests, to a point in which customers can be made to feel negligent—as if they are shirking their social responsibilities—if they do not submit ratings. What had once been truly voluntary and peripheral to the customer-employee transaction has become increasingly coerced and central. Significantly, the most dramatic example of the growing use of customer ratings can be seen in the so-called "sharing economy" or, due to its greater precision, what I will refer to as the "on-demand economy," which has additionally been called "collaborative consumption," "platform economy," "gig economy," "access economy," and "crowd-based capitalism," among other monikers (Yaraghi and Ravi 2017; Sundararajan 2016).

The on-demand economy, which is expected to grow from 14 billion dollars in 2014 to 335 billion dollars by 2025 (Yaraghi and Ravi 2017), has been characterized as a system of peer-to-peer exchange via decentralized, typically online, platforms. The on-demand economy is not as monolithic as it sounds but is instead comprised of multiple business models, including economic powerhouses in which participants buy and sell rather than "share" services (e.g., Uber, Lyft, and Airbnb) as well as a declining number of generally smaller networks in which there are either limited or no financial exchanges between members who can share, barter, or in some cases rent services or goods (e.g., Couchsurfing, Neighborgoods, and, for some services, Craigslist). Among other things, companies facilitate rides (e.g., Uber, Lyft, Gett, and SideCar), car sharing (e.g., Getaround), bicycle sharing (e.g., Liquid), freelance "gigs" (e.g., TaskRabbit, Upwork, and Zaarly), dog-sitting (e.g., Dogvacay), used clothes-selling (e.g., Poshmark and threadUP), and lodging (Airbnb and Hospitality Club).

The on-demand economy has received copious criticism, some of which is focused on the fact that, since its heyday circa 2010, it has become steadily absorbed into the dominant, decidedly nonsharing, economy (Kessler 2015). The optimism that predicted a more humane, egalitarian, and environmentally friendly economy less than a decade ago now seems, amid the collapse of countless non-profits and the consolidation of a handful of for-profit behemoths, quaint or naïve. Critics have also looked at the ways in which the dominant, or Uber, sector of the on-demand economy has prospered specifically through the mass influx of venture capital and the intensification of labor exploitation (Scholz ed. 2013; Asher-Schapiro 2014; Roose 2014; Kessler 2015). Certainly for all but the most cynical free-market propagandists, it is undeniable that drivers for services such as Uber and Lyft are severely exploited. The putative autonomy that these companies offer their workers—many of whom have been forced into piecemeal, part-time work due to the dearth of well-paying full-time jobs—is more than offset by what frequently amounts to subminimum wage earnings and the requirement that drivers use their own vehicles and pay for their own insurance, maintenance, and gas (Asher-Schapiro 2014). These ridesharing companies additionally have little interest in providing any semblance of security or benefits to workers who they self-servingly classify as "independent contractors." In fact, some such jobs may soon become obsolete due to the increasing availability of self-driving cars (Marshall 2017).

Because labor is a chief cost of business, it is tempting to assume that high levels of labor exploitation, although unfortunate, can at least be partially justified because of the benefits such lowered costs provide to the consumer. Even critics who have condemned the on-demand economy as a serf-run "concierge economy" concede that companies such as Uber have created new standards of convenience for consumers (Naughton 2014).[4] However, this bad-for-the worker/good-for-the-consumer dichotomy can distract us not only from the fact that consumers are of course also workers but also from the ways in which certain business practices can be bad for both the worker *and* the consumer.

The economic model used by the most successful on-demand companies is significantly based on dramatic cost reduction achieved through the elimination of traditional management. Specifically, these companies have streamlined modern business practices through reassigning traditionally managerial duties—including monitoring, directing, and disciplining workers—to unpaid, or crowdsourced, customers. Although consumer management, as noted, is not new, it has historically been a subsidiary and largely informal practice. The on-demand economy has exponentially expanded and institutionalized it, incorporating customers into the production process on a scale that would have been previously unimaginable.

The generally unregulated, peer-to-peer transactions that are a staple of the on-demand economy require that participants trust one another. The key mechanism for establishing such trust is the availability of public reviews commending or condemning potential collaborators, encouraging participants to act honorably if only to safeguard their public reputations and, with them, their ability to continue operating on a given platform. However, there is evidence that these ratings are less reliable than presumed. For instance, a study of six hundred thousand Airbnb listings found that over 95 percent are 4.5 or 5 and nearly none has a rating of under 3.5 (Zervas, Proserpio, and Byers 2015; Slee 2016; see also Slee 2014). Noting that nearly 99 percent of all drivers on BlaBlaCar, a French ride-hailing company, have perfect ratings, Tom Slee observes that ratings do not "meaningfully discriminate among drivers or riders" (Slee 2013). Similarly, Uber and Lyft can deactivate drivers whose ratings fall below 4.7, leading to a system in which nearly every driver is highly rated.[5] Such unreliability possibly reflects the fact that customers—in contrast to the highly motivated, or genuinely voluntary, reviewers on sites such as Yelp and RMP—are posting their ratings with little consideration other than to complete an imposed, even if not technically required, task. The existence of disproportionately high ratings might also reflect a common desire to avoid confrontation, feelings of guilt resulting from presumably harming someone's professional well-being, or retaliation (Slee 2014). Uber, Lyft, and Airbnb (which we might refer to as the Big Three) in fact mandate that workers (or "hosts") rate customers, who in turn have to concern themselves with protecting their own reputations lest they are denied future service. It is quite telling that customers are not asked whether they want to rate workers and are given no power to opt out of being rated themselves, doing much violence to the notion of the "sovereign consumer." And it is notable that while workers and customers are busily rating one another neither group is asked to rate the CEOs and investors who are profiting at their expense.

As in other industries, peer-to-peer companies are able to determine who qualifies as a customer, and thereby gets to be rated, in the first place. Significantly, there is substantial evidence indicating that the on-demand economy discriminates against customers on the basis of sex and race. On eBay, men consistently receive higher prices than do women selling comparable items (Bohannon 2016), while women are more likely to be overcharged, or taken on longer rides, on Uber and Lyft than are men (Ge, Knittel, MacKenzie, and Zoepf 2016). Meanwhile, studies in Seattle and Boston show that Uber and Lyft drivers are more than twice as likely to cancel rides with men with African American–sounding names or pictures (Lyft, but not Uber, shows drivers pictures of prospective passengers) than with men with white-sounding names (and it is not unreasonable to imagine that such drivers will give lower ratings to the African American riders—presumably ones with non-African American–sounding names—who they do pick up, putting African Americans at even greater risk of being excluded from service in the on-demand economy) (Fisman and Luca 2016; Ramaswamy 2017). As a result, African Americans hailing rides on Uber or Lyft in Seattle wait up to 35 percent longer than do white riders (Ge, Knittel, MacKenzie, and Zoepf 2016). Similarly, Airbnb hosts are 16 percent likelier to reject guests with African American–sounding names than ones with white-sounding names (Edelman and Luca 2014; Ramaswamy 2017).

To be sure, it is well-known that traditional taxi drivers have historically discriminated against African American riders, so Uber and Lyft are hardly unique in this regard. However, racist discrimination within the on-demand economy—and here Airbnb is more illustrative—nevertheless points to the ways in which institutional racism can become collectivized and thereby more intractable. The federal government following the 1964 Civil Rights Act has, often successfully, sought to curtail racist discrimination by business providers. Attempting to prosecute such discrimination today not among businesses per se but their myriad of independent contractors presents a more unwieldy and onerous task, a virtual game of whack-a-mole in which structural—as opposed to attitudinal—racism has migrated from the institution to the individual.

The case of African Americans is, again, instructive of the weakness of all consumers under capitalism in general and within the burgeoning on-demand economy in particular. African Americans have historically occupied a uniquely vulnerable position not only within the labor force ("first fired, last hired") but also within consumer society. The persistence of such racism has, among other things, functioned to help conceal the existence of an inherently exploitative economic system through drawing attention to and frequently blaming its victims rather than its structural causes. Racism can thereby mystify consumer weakness insofar as free-market apologists tend to claim that the market would work fairly *if not for* its corruption via exogenous factors such as racism; *it's all of us, not capitalism, that is to blame*. In reality, as this book emphasizes, capitalism's creation of winners (e.g., those who have access to seemingly anything and everything) necessitates the production of losers (e.g., those who, excluded themselves, must provide this access to others). Racism, which produces a visible and discrete population whose economic exploitation is likelier to be socially and politically sanctioned, meshes perfectly with such a system.

As noted earlier, even in a world in which prejudices such as racism and sexism were eliminated, our intrinsically competitive economic system would almost certainly engender new discriminatory practices with which to stratify and regulate not only people in general, based on uneven ownership of property, but consumers in particular. Similarly, through thinking about those on-demand companies that, unlike the Big Three, have been characterized as "gift economies" (e.g., Couchsurfing, Hospitality Club, aspects of Craigslist, and, to some extent, Neighborgoods) we can identify the structural weakness of consumers even in the best of circumstances (Sundararajan 2016, 38).

We should first point out that insofar as they are based on anticipated reciprocity, exchanges through "gift economy" platforms are in fact not gifts at all but instead constitute bartering (Sundararajan, 36). David Graeber, following Caroline Humphrey (1985), has shown that contrary to popular mythology barter-based societies have never existed in practice, and when pre-industrial societies did barter it generally took place between groups that considered one another foreign or hostile (Graeber 2011). Such bartering could be fraught with danger, and the fundamental antagonism of interests underlying it was, in Graeber's account, often expressed through ritualized displays of aggression and play. In coordinating our reliance on strangers—individuals who in previous eras would have quite possibly been considered enemies—the "sharing economy" in fact reminds us of both our dependence on extended reliable and trusted communities and their disappearance from much of modern life.

Even hospitality networks—in which travelers and hosts exchange free lodging—exist within a setting that is profoundly conditioned by capitalism. Such networks therefore tend to reproduce, as much as ameliorate, capitalism's characteristically fraught social relations. Some hosts on the Couchsurfing platform decide to share their homes not in return for access to future boarding themselves but because they seek company, evoking the isolation that drove many women to visit department stores in earlier eras (Davies 2014). Notably, some of these hosts are disappointed to discover that their guests are often less interested in socializing with them than in staying out late and treating their would-be compatriots like random hostel managers, illustrating not only the prevalence of loneliness in our society but also the difficulty in overcoming it (Davies 2014; Steylaerts and Dubhghaill 2012). Simultaneously, there are guests, some who have limited resources and are thereby highly dependent on their hosts, who have complained about the social demands that hosts place on them, with one writing: "(Couchsurfing) is not free, you are selling your freedom to your host" (Davies 2014). The "gift" in these cases is therefore exchanged by people in positions of socially produced vulnerability—loneliness and a need for housing, respectively—who in fact expect personal benefits in return.[6] Similarly, the existence of childcare swapping platforms (e.g., Sitting Around) reveals tremendous social want, as it would have been unthinkable in societies with extended families and communal networks (that is, society for the mass majority of human history) that one would have had to worry about finding caregivers, strangers no less, to tend to one's children. To be sure, contemporary childcare sharing precedes the digital revolution, although much of it notably has occurred in poor and working-class communities in which heightened cooperation is in part a response to more limited resources and higher levels of unemployment. The growing popularity of such community exchanges—we should also remember that during the Depression struggling families frequently generated income through renting out parts of their homes to boarders—demonstrates not the growth of a socialist or otherwise post-market society but the democratization of poverty within capitalism.

Indeed, the ongoing impoverishment of the dwindling middle-class coincides with the exponential expansion of unfathomable fortunes controlled by a miniscule proportion of the population. Demanding a fairer system, some observers have called for more equal distribution of the on-demand economy's soaring profits (see Schor 2014). However, the emphasis on more equitable redistribution of profit risks neglecting the circumstances in which these services are being provided in the first place, circumstances shaped by socially produced want and, frequently, economic desperation. There is nothing natural or inevitable in the fact that people are in need of, say, childcare, and there is nothing laudable in the fact that so many people are willing to—we might more accurately say forced to—drive strangers all over town in an effort to make ends meet in an increasingly unforgiving and demanding economy. Such activities, Ivan Illich reminds us in his analysis of shadow work, are indeed necessary for sustaining the formal economy (people, after all, have to get to their jobs), but they are hardly necessary for the subsistence of human beings in general (Illich 1981, 8). Meeting these needs through the on-demand economy does demonstrate that we are connecting with one another, but such connections are no less designed to, first and foremost, subsidize the system of capitalism.

While much of the on-demand economy is based on financial or nonfinancial exchange (e.g., bartering), there is one area in which it does appear to function as a gift economy, which brings us back to our online consumer managers. Consumers who go out of their way to write unpaid reviews—including not only on Yelp and RMP but also on sites such as WebMD and Amazon—do appear to be offering gifts with no expectation of return. The social value of gift-giving within gift economies, it has been noted, less involves the substance of the gift than the reinforcement of social connection and mutual obligation that the act of giving cultivates (Sundararajan 2016, 36–37 [Sundararajan is building on the analysis of Lewis Hyde]). Nevertheless, even if we subordinate the content of the gift to the increased connection that giving it fosters, we still ought to interrogate the basis of such connections.

The gift of online reviews is not offered to just anyone and everyone, to society as such. Rather, reviews are written for the specific benefit of fellow consumers. Insofar as such gift-giving generates feelings of warmth and solidarity, then, they are feelings that come at the expense of workers who, as we will see, are regulated and disciplined through such reviews. Such gift-giving therefore produces meaning not through increasing the unity of the whole society but, on the contrary, through increasing social antagonisms *within* society. Such gift-giving is also frequently profitable for the owners of the online platforms on which it occurs, illustrating another unique characteristic of this form of activity: that is, before it can benefit its recipients, it must provide an expectation of profit to an intermediary, an illustration of the growing practical requirement that popular acts of selflessness and camaraderie be, above all, profitable.

NOTES

1. I use the terms consumer management and customer management interchangeably.
2. YouTube, for instance, shares small, often miniscule, proportions of earnings with its contributors.
3. Yelp, as discussed in chapter 3, was nevertheless in its early stages redesigned to reflect the (assuredly profitable) desires of site users who were primarily interested in writing reviews, indicating that the contemporary producer-consumer relationship, although unequal, should hardly be thought of as unilateral.
4. To be sure, some critics have also addressed some of the largely unregulated on-demand economy's harmful effects on consumers (see, for instance, Baker 2014).
5. The existence of high ratings should not necessarily be equated with good service as such, as accumulated high ratings can in fact provide drivers with the leverage to provide periodic inferior service if they so desire.
6. Whereas profiles and referrals regulate the site, it is difficult to confidently anticipate how guests and hosts will get along in person due to factors such as unreciprocated attraction and situational fatigue.

Chapter Two

How the Consumer Was Invented (and Is Being Reinvented)

There have been numerous accounts, both scholarly and popular, of the apparent disintegration of the boundary separating workers and consumers. Indeed, the neologism "prosumer," coined by Alvin Toffler (1980), is increasingly used to describe the informal, unpaid labor that consumers routinely perform. While prosumption has existed for decades—for instance, in the form of selecting and bagging our own groceries, bussing our tables in fast-food restaurants, filling our gas tanks, and building our own furniture—the emergence of the Internet has exponentially increased the practice, and it now constitutes a far greater proportion of our daily lives. Much of today's Internet (or Web 2.0) consists of websites composed of content produced by users themselves. Whether uploading dating profiles on Match.com, photos and articles on Facebook, résumés on LinkedIn, comments on the *New York Times*, or customer reviews on Amazon, millions of Internet users spend untold hours producing the content that makes the Internet possible and profitable. While these prosumers have a great many motives and frequently derive personal satisfaction from their efforts, these forms of prosumption nevertheless generate wealth that its creators are excluded from. Although such unremunerated wealth does not constitute formal exploitation insofar as prosumers are not wage laborers, there is one form of prosumption that can in fact increase wage laborers' surplus value and thereby generate profit and overall economic growth. Online customer management, which intensifies work for wage earners, is both a unique form of prosumption and, I argue, its quintessential expression.

While the following chapters examine two case studies of online consumer management, this chapter looks at how we arrived at the current historical moment, one in which it is part of normal life that millions of people participate in providing wealth-generating labor, as well as monetizable personal data, for which they are not remunerated. That is, more than ever, consumers work, although with no boss to complain to or job to quit, it is work that is more often than not naturalized as merely a part of the demands of "life" (e.g., the professional obligation to maintain a LinkedIn account) or voluntarily embraced as personally (though not financially) enriching interaction within an otherwise often isolating society. This chapter is not intended to function as a comprehensive history of the consumer, an enormous and multifaceted subject with an equally enormous literature. Rather, it broadly maps one particular trajectory of development—the consumer as worker and, ultimately, manager—examining key themes, turning points, and illustrative moments along the way.[1] In particular, I use the concepts of exploitation and alienation to both chart the consumer's evolution within an ever more sophisticated capitalism and to assess the implications of prosumption in general and online consumer management in particular.

The story that follows is premised on two related theoretical observations by Marx concerning the unique character of capitalism. While all historic economic systems preceding capitalism were based on the production of items for use, capitalism, based on profit, produces items for exchange. In chapter 4 of *Capital* Marx (1992 [1867]) describes this transformation by noting that in prior economic systems the circulation of commodities via money had an endpoint when a buyer received a desired commodity (or C-M-C), whereas in capitalism it is money itself that is circulated via (other) commodities so that more money can return to an investor, accumulating with no endpoint (or M-C-M). Because the accumulation of capital has no end, capitalists require that there always exists effective demand, that is, moneyed consumers who need or desire what is being produced. Although humans have of course been consuming since the species emerged, the particular form of consumption required to sustain capitalism has only come into being with the advent of capitalist production. In the *Grundrisse* Marx (1993 [1939]) notes that production itself entails consumption, "just as natural procreation is a consumption of life forces" (90). Simultaneously, consumption entails production, for example, through eating, in which humans consume while producing their bodies. Marx indicates that production and consumption are then not only one another's opposite but also always mediate each other, a general phenomenon that takes on particular implications within an economic system based on exchange value. Production creates both the material for consumption as well as consumption's "specificity, its character, its finish" (92). The object is never a general object but a specific one that must be consumed in a particular fashion. "Hunger is hunger, but the hunger gratified by cooked meat eaten with a knife and fork is a different hunger from that which bolts down raw meat with the aid of hand, nail, and tooth. Production thus produces not only the object but also the manner of consumption, not only objectively but subjectively. Production thus creates the consumer" (92). It is further consumers' very perception of objects—once consumption has evolved from its initial stages—that creates consumers' need for them. Thus, "production not only supplies a material for the need, but it also supplies a need for the material" (92). Consumption then also mediates production, supplying to production the subjects—or "finishing touch"—that products need to become real: "A house where no one lives is in fact not a real house" (91). If production provides the object, consumption provides the subject, a dialectic whose material impetus and initiative nevertheless reside with production, which shapes and reshapes the consumer all the while being dependent on it.

Informed by Marx's description of the symbiotic though disparate relationship between production and consumption under capitalism, I trace below three stages in the evolution of the modern consumer inside of the United States. While it is important to note that different countries had different paths of development (e.g., countries with higher degrees of working-class consciousness and organization, such as Italy and the United Kingdom, were not coincidentally characterized by what we can describe as a delayed and initially less fervent consumer culture), this study focuses specifically on the United States, in which the relatively early development of a mass, individualistic, competitive, and racialized consumer culture can be viewed as a precocious, and in some instances maximalist, exemplar of contemporary global capitalism. The first stage of this development occurred roughly between 1880–1945 and entails the invention of modern consumers, who were in their infancy introduced to mass advertising and national brands and learned how to navigate shopping routines that we have come to often think of as natural. The second stage occurred between 1945–1973, an era of unprecedented economic expansion in which the standard of living significantly increased for large numbers of people while greater demands were placed on consumers who—maturing through the adoption of new customs and the internalization of new norms—were increasingly asked to more formally assist in the production process itself. The third stage began with the collapse of the postwar boom in 1973 and has exponentially accelerated with the growth of the Internet. Strained growth from the 1970s onward has placed downward pressure on profit, leading to stagnant wages (supplemented by personal credit) and more ambitious, increasingly intellectual, demands on consumers culminating in new forms of prosumption and customer management. While the demands placed on consumers have quantitatively and qualitatively evolved in relation to both the structural changes in the global economy and the consumer's internalization of consumerist ideologies, the fundamental role of the consumer has not. Although this story is hardly linear or teleological, we can nonetheless identify the unique kernel of the capitalist system of production inside of today's consumer manager.

BORN WEAK: THE INVENTION OF THE MODERN CONSUMER

In order to understand contemporary prosumption, we need to first revisit the origins and evolution of consumer society itself, a society in which "for the first time in history, the working population . . . worked entirely for wages, and obtained material necessities and luxuries entirely through purchases in the marketplace" (Goodwin, Ackerman, and Kiron 1997, 115).

At their broadest, debates on modern consumption feature a foundational split over the origins of consumer society, specifically concerning whether its impetus was the quantitative and qualitative increase in production during the Industrial Revolution or the growth of consumer demand itself. Neil McKendrick (1982), advancing the latter view, argues that a consumer revolution was the precondition for the revolution in production, noting that radical works spanning the eighteenth century (from Mandeville's *Fable of the Bees* to Adam Smith's *Wealth of Nations*) overturned thousands of years of Christian teachings that equated parsimoniousness with virtue as well as the mercantilist axiom that national wealth was generated through a favorable balance of trade and an accompanying policy of beggaring thy neighbor (McKendrick 1982; Goodwin, Ackerman, and Kiron 1997). Following the intellectual break sanctioning what came to be known as conspicuous consumption, the wealthy commissioned the construction of extravagant homes, filled them with opulent furniture, porcelain, pottery, silver, and mirrors, planted exotic gardens, and obsessively pursued new fashions. The middle classes, and eventually everybody else, followed as best they could the examples set by the rich, and this "social emulation" produced enormous aggregate demand that became the "engine" of mass production, brought luxuries to more people than ever before, and fundamentally transformed the economic system (see also Veblen 1994 [1899]; Holt 2000; Bourdieu 1984; Simmel 1957 [1904], and Warner, Meeker, and Eells, 1949).

Ben Fine and Ellen Leopold challenge McKendrick's contention that consumer demand can be understood as an independent cause of economic and social transformation, and instead assert that demand, as in Say's dictum, is instead an effect of supply (Fine and Leopold 1990; Goodwin, Ackerman, and Kiron 1997).[2] Specifically, Fine and Leopold reject McKendrick's description of social emulation. Rather than trying to mimic the fashions of their social "betters," servants, the authors note, typically inherited their employers' unwanted clothing, which they would have been unable to afford and arguably uninterested in purchasing even if they could. Fine and Leopold additionally note that many goods, for instance coal, exist outside of the pressures of social emulation altogether.

This debate over the roots of consumer society mirrors the field of economics' debate concerning whether capitalism is characterized by a primacy of production or consumption. Classical political economic thinkers including Adam Smith and Karl Marx viewed consumption as an effect of the productive sphere. Although Smith asserted that the sole purpose of production is the well-being of the consumer, he famously explained that capitalism benefits the consumer in a decidedly roundabout manner. That is, the increased efficiency and lowered prices created through capitalist competition can only benefit consumers if the state limits its interference in production and paradoxically enables individuals to pursue their own private interests. Marx's explication of capitalism emphasizes the primacy of the social and economic relations embedded in private property, namely, the fact that capitalists monopolize the means of production through which wage laborers must work. Because wages tend to rise amid capitalist competition, the proportion of profit, or surplus value, that capitalists extract from workers inevitably declines, encouraging capitalists to replace workers with machines. Here, however, capitalists ironically but unavoidably undermine their ability to generate surplus value that only living labor can provide, and capitalists' efforts to reduce costs, while increasing productivity, degenerate into a vicious cycle of further declining profit and crisis.

While the classical political economists drew different conclusions, their general emphasis on production has important implications for understanding capitalism as well as the causes of, and thereby solutions to, its crises. Although turn-of-the-century economists who advocated laissez-faire asserted that capitalist crises correct themselves if left alone, John Maynard Keynes, focusing on the social and political implications of the Great Depression, famously noted that "in the long run we're all dead." Keynes profoundly challenged prevailing economic thought by arguing that economic crises can be resolved by fueling consumer demand. The New Deal sought to directly—e.g., via Social Security—and indirectly—e.g., via government jobs and increased unionization—put money into consumers' pockets. Yet, significantly, it was not until the massive military spending generated by WWII that the great slump came to an end. Economists therefore debate whether the New Deal failed to end the Depression because consumer spending was still not large enough to eliminate the glut in production or because the government's creation and redistribution of money could not in itself provide the value money achieves through profitable investment in private enterprise. By contrast, the government's prodigious consumption of military goods beginning with the Lend-Lease Act provided a more reliable basis for the realization of money's value and growth. Not only did government spending directly support the private sector, where surplus value can be produced in contrast to the non-profit public sector, but the regular use and obsolescence of military equipment were also particularly amenable to profit in ways that, for instance, the construction of public schools and the painting of murals were not.

Although Keynesian policies achieved the dominant status previously enjoyed by laissez-faire, as the latter was discredited by its failure to both predict the Great Depression and propose any effective response to it, Keynesianism itself had become exhausted after 1973, as a new round of global glut, dramatically increasing oil prices, and the new phenomenon of stagflation put a decisive end to the long postwar boom. As Labor Prime Minister James Callaghan complained, "'We used to think that you could just spend your way out of a recession . . . I tell you, in all candour, that that option no longer exists'" (Judt 2005). Keynesianism's decline, however, did not lead, as is sometimes assumed, to the simple resuscitation of laissez-faire, which had been defended during the 1950s and 1960s primarily by largely ignored true believers such as Ludwig von Mises, Friedrich Hayek, and Milton Friedman. Although new arenas of profit were in fact created through devouring the Keynesian welfare state via tax cuts, privatization, and deregulation, post-1973 political-economy, or neoliberalism, counterintuitively consisted of the further abandonment of laissez-faire—albeit in a different manner from that of the New Deal. Specifically, neoliberalism entailed, as Foucault has argued, a transformation in governance resulting in the expansion and *marketization* of the political sphere (Foucault 2010). Particularly significant for Foucault is that neoliberal theorists, and increasingly states, recognized that competition is not some innate tendency awaiting release but is instead a "structure with formal properties" useful for regulating the economy:

> Consequently, if competition really was this formal structure, both rigorous in its internal structure but fragile in its real, historical existence, then the problem of liberal policy was precisely to develop in fact the concrete and real space in which the formal structure of competition could function. . . . Neoliberalism should not therefore be identified with laissez-faire, but rather with permanent vigilance, activity, and intervention (Foucault 2010, 131–32).

We might then say that even if consumption *were* the engine of capitalist growth, consumption under capitalism is nevertheless substantially shaped and conditioned by institutions that are external to it.

Indeed, arguments that treat consumer demand as an independent variable in the development of capitalism tend to downplay consumer demand's unique historic preconditions. Specifically, the critical prerequisite for the emergence of consumers was their forced removal from what they want and need (most notoriously through the Enclosure Acts and European colonialism), and this exclusion, which can only be mitigated with money and thereby (for the mass majority) wage labor, is maintained through enormous military and political force (Polanyi 2001 [1944], Part II). In other words, irrespective of whether consumer society was created by producers or consumers, and apart from consumers' disadvantages such as capitalists' use of planned obsolescence and other strategies designed to extract unending profit, the consumer, defined by lack and need, was born weak.

If this point is self-evident, it is nevertheless infrequently emphasized in the literature on what has been termed the "Consumerist Turn" or the "Fordist Deal." Lawrence Glickman (1999) has shown how in the late nineteenth century and early twentieth century labor leaders came to accept the rule of wage labor, previously condemned per se as "wage slavery," in exchange for a putative "American standard of living" that would provide workers with wages high enough to access the growing variety of goods being produced by the market system provided that these workers were unionized, white, and male. Similarly, Gabriel and Lang have discussed Henry Ford's decision to pay his workers relatively high wages so that they could purchase his automobiles: "Ford offered his workforce the carrot of material enjoyment outside the workplace as compensation for the de-skilling, control and alienation that imposed in the workplace" (2015 [1995], 10). Aside from the fact that Ford, amid intense competition, later reversed his decision and lowered wages, the description of a compromise in which the toil of wage labor would be offset by the benefits of consumption minimizes consumption's numerous downsides—not least the unpaid work that consumers must continually perform.

Ford's payment of high wages was of course contingent upon the assumption that workers would spend them on Ford cars. While Ford's employees were in fact free to spend, or not spend, their money where they chose, Ford nonetheless recognized that under capitalism, unlike the economic systems that preceded it, the role of production is not to meet consumers' needs but to earn profit—and thereby enable ever more production. Instead of producing so that we can consume, under capitalism we consume so that we can produce, or as economist Robert R. Nathan succinctly puts it, "'Mass consumption is essential to the success of a system of mass production'" (Cohen 2003, 116).[3] Consumers are therefore left with the responsibility of not only meeting their own needs but also sustaining the system of production itself, a point made explicit with the implementation of Keynesianism and, more recently, the George W. Bush administration's formal identification of shopping with patriotism following 9/11.

In fact, the exponential expansion of mass production during the Industrial Revolution, facilitated through new and far more rapid communication and transportation technologies, required that both consumer demand and consumers themselves be manufactured. This was in many ways a contrived and often onerous process that was neither organic nor inevitable but was instead frequently planned and executed by powerful businesses and the state. A "crisis in the control of consumer demand," as James Beniger describes it, emerged in the 1880s as new "continuous processing technologies" dramatically increased the production of a wide range of commodities—from canned foods to cigarettes to oats—requiring vastly expanded, predictable, and consistent demand lest the increasingly capital intensive new economy implode from glut (1986, 264). Confronting only an incipient, unstable, and highly heterogeneous market, the new mass producers, irrespective of practices of "social emulation," turned to market research in order to "construct" consumers "who could be managed with advertising and other units of the marketer's arsenal" (Zwick, Bonsu, and Darmody 2008, 169).[4] That is, market research "emerged not as a means of seeking consumer input, but as a social process for managing consumers, reducing marketing complexities, and improving production efficiencies . . ." (Zwick, Bonsu, and Darmody 2008, 169). In other words, capitalists' control of industrial production (e.g., through interchangeable parts, size standardization, and the assembly line) and labor (e.g., through Taylorist scientific management of workers' movements) ultimately extended to consumers themselves (Beniger 1986, 294). That consumers today increasingly volunteer their own product preferences and personal data to marketers (for instance, via Facebook "likes" and Pinterest "pins") suggests the extent to which consumers have begun to, in effect, regulate themselves.

The case of the late nineteenth-century increase in oat production is instructive of how the requirements of production determine the forms of consumption. Beniger (1986, 220) describes a miller who in 1882 incorporated new productive processing technologies and soon produced twice the amount of oats that was then being purchased in the nation annually. Although oats had until then been largely disparaged as a food source primarily suitable for horses, a widespread and aggressive advertising campaign helped convince millions of consumers to begin eating oatmeal as a morning meal. The point of course is not to make normative claims regarding the merits of oatmeal but to demonstrate how the needs of capitalists radically reshaped society's conceptions and habits. Consumers did not demand that oatmeal be produced. Instead, new technologies enabled the cheap mass production of oatmeal, and consumers were then successfully convinced to incorporate it into their diets. Consumers were of course free to reject oatmeal as a suitable food item, but such consumer choice had no control over what was produced in the first place. Rather than reflecting market demand, "'Items to be manufactured were designed and selected for production according to how quickly and economically they could be produced. In place of the naïve consumer, the 'scientific' system now made its own demands'" (Beniger 1986, 299).[5]

Notably, business leaders did not use advertising solely to direct and increase consumer demand but also to wage price wars with competitors and to battle wholesalers and merchants who controlled distribution channels. Capitalists are, of course, not monolithic. Nevertheless, they frequently have converging interests and assumptions regarding the consumer. Through the use of techniques including advertising, trademarking, branding, and packaging, capitalists used consumers to compel wholesalers to distribute their products and force retailers—who had hitherto dealt in generics whose origins were not identifiable to consumers—to shelve and display them according to producers' preferences (Beniger 1986, chapters 7 and 8). Thus, even the hallmark of consumer power—the power to choose among products—was from the beginning of consumer society cultivated and exploited by manufacturers seeking to wrest control from retailers and other rivals along the chain of distribution. This process was reversed decades later when retailers, led by Walmart, regained control from producers through the use of, among other techniques, customer self-service and the collection of point-of-sale consumer data via barcodes (Lichtenstein 2009). Throughout these battles, the consumer functioned, in many respects, as little more than a pawn.

For instance, when visiting stores near the turn of the century customers increasingly found themselves in spaces that had been carefully designed to control their movements in order to encourage them to consume what they otherwise would not. Describing the first Piggy Wiggly market, Beniger (1986, 333–34) writes:

> (Clarence) Saunders's essential idea was to process neither transactions nor commodities as his primary retail function but rather customers themselves. His first Piggy Wiggly store, opened in 1916, was explicitly designed to process people past merchandise. Turnstiles channeled entering customers into a single aisle, where they could do little else but advance back and forth through a maze of shelves, past all items in stock (packaged, of course, to "sell themselves"), until they reached the exit turnstile, complete with a check-out counter and cash register—and the only employee then at work in the store. Saunders's scheme, what he called a "self-serving" store, can be found to this day in retail establishments throughout the world.

Although consumers would eventually become more skillful in navigating the commercial spaces that increasingly shaped their lives, such savviness was born of continual effort to discern the meaning and effects of advertising and other forms of commercial manipulation as well as endless trial and error in experimenting with, frequently cheap or defective, products themselves. To be sure, not all consumers are the same, and they therefore do not all pay equivalent prices for lessons in learning how to consume.

KEEPING UP WITH THE JONESES . . . OR KEEPING THE JONESES DOWN?

The category of consumers is, under capitalism, inherently exclusionary. One can only consume if one has money, but money is not evenly distributed under a system based on private property and competition. Notably, the U.S. labor leaders who embraced the consumerist turn identified themselves—and the other unionized white males whom they represented—as elite members atop a rigid hierarchy of workers, ones with the bearing, responsibility, and taste to consume responsibly (Glickman 1999, 85–91). These leaders, mirroring the particular historic social stratifications of the United States, saw consumption through a pronouncedly racialized and gendered worldview. Labor leaders such as Samuel Gompers, George Gunton, and Thomas Armstrong viewed laborers and consumers in explicitly racial terms, for instance castigating the Chinese for consuming too little (Glickman 1999, 85–91). According to Glickman, the Chinese were said to be not '"true consumers"' (88), but instead, as noted by Armstrong, people who:

> [T]ake out of circulation daily the sum of seventy-five thousand dollars. . . . They trade and traffic entirely with themselves. They spend none of the money they earn with the white merchants of the city. . . . They can live on five cents a day; they eat rice and the offal of the slaughter-houses and we are inclined to think they eat something worse in the shape of vermin.

At the same time, African Americans were criticized for consuming too much. Gompers, according to Glickman (1999, 90), described the 1917 St. Louis Race Riots by noting that '"East St. Louis became a sort of convention center for excited, undisciplined negroes who were intoxicated by higher wages than they had ever known."' Thus, consumers must fulfill their needs and circulate their earnings in the greater economy, but these must be '"civilized needs"' befitting responsible, restrained, white, Christian, breadwinners (88). Being a consumer meant knowing how to "consume properly" (88), a revealingly fluid concept that defined itself against the behavior of those purportedly either too slavish and uncivilized or too childlike and undisciplined to don the mantle, and enjoy the higher wages accompanying it, of "consumer."

The notion of consuming "properly" for the labor leaders of the early twentieth century contrasted with the earlier ideals of the self-denial and frugality described in both Weber's *Protestant Work Ethic* (2002 [1905]) and Franklin's *Poor Richard's Almanac* (1759) as well as the "conspicuous consumption," initially described in Veblen's *Theory of the Leisure Class* (1899), that had by the postwar period increasingly influenced the middle class. In all these conceptualizations, however, the notion of the consumer is inherently relational, defined by the negative examples of what it is not (see also Holt 2000; Bourdieu 1984; Simmel 1957 [1904]; Warner, Meeker, and Eells 1949). That the conventional understanding of what it means to be a "good consumer" is continually evolving suggests that the insecurity that characterizes success in employment due to economic competition also characterizes success in consumption due to, in this instance, social competition. And maintaining such success, once it was no longer restricted to white, male, labor elites, required not only money but also the time and effort needed to perpetually learn and fulfill continually shifting expectations that include but go well beyond what to buy and what not to buy.

Thus, it is accurate in the abstract but ultimately misleading to account for consumerism by referring to consumers' personal motives to merely acquire commodities or even their desire to get ahead at the expense of others. It is more precise to say that consumers exist within a fundamentally competitive social-economic context in which they have good reason, as Veblen understood, to continually fear *falling behind*. Analogous to the ways in which nineteenth-century whites disdained wage labor precisely because performing such work could blur the distinction between whites and Black slaves, turn of the century white male consumers feared that "improper" consumption would blur categories distancing them from both the "lesser races" and the dependent, domestic women they wielded control over at home. While the racist and sexist categories composing the hierarchy of consumers were by no means transcended in the postwar era, the relative socioeconomic ascension of many women and people of color nonetheless helps illuminate the hierarchy's fixed base: the lower class, which is collectively represented in consumer culture as undesirable per se (Bourdieu 1984).

The notion of the poor, whether racialized or deemed mere "white trash," helps constitute the static "them" that consumers—with an agency in the socially symbolic world that workers often lack in the economic world—strive to distance themselves from, reflecting the belief that vulnerability to the stigma of capitalist penury can be transcended through acquiring the accoutrements of not relative material wealth per se but relative symbolic wealth.[6] We should be careful not to suggest, however, that there exists some ahistorical gap wholly separating the material from the symbolic. In his response to Veblen, Adorno notes that nineteenth-century ostentation "might well stem from the necessity to depict oneself as a good risk with a high credit rating. This necessity could reflect the scarcity of capital during periods of expansion" (Adorno 1984 [1967], 78).

It is precisely through observing the relationship between the material and the symbolic that we can understand the fear of falling behind, which can be heard in the mockery ritually accorded to obsolete commodities (e.g., eight-tracks, cassettes, VHS tapes, flip-phones, and fashions such as bell-bottom jeans, parachute pants, the wrong shoes, the wrong glasses, the wrong haircut [before it becomes the right haircut again], and so on).[7] The struggle to stay out in front is costly and endless, as it entails perpetually acquiring, and reacquiring, the ephemeral cultural capital required to apprehend semiotic wealth (Bourdieu 1984; Holt 2000; Simmel 1957 [1904]). This struggle cannot end as long as there is capitalism insofar as the continual threat of social obsolescence reflects the reality that anybody can become poor.

However, there is another, affirmative, component of consumerism in that it is a response to the alienation created in part by the Industrial Revolution's removal of people from direct access to the necessities of life and its imposition of a rigid division of labor. While the former can be remedied through purchasing what one needs and wants (albeit typically with money earned from alienated labor) the latter is more intractable. Consumerism of course does not remedy alienation by returning us to a less atomized preindustrial life but rather enables entirely new forms of community, albeit ones that frequently reproduce the relations that help produce alienation in the first place.

The changes that many women experienced following the Industrial Revolution are emblematic of the alienation caused by industrial society in general. One need not romanticize the gender relations of prendustrial life to note that the traditional division of labor had dramatically intensified as men not only began working in factories outside the home but also received wages and, with them, social approval for their work. Women then not only went frequently without pay—or at best, so to speak, with lower pay—but additionally inherited a higher proportion of the work and responsibilities in and around the home.

Although it is often assumed that middle- and upper-class women homemakers were beneficiaries of the new time-saving and energy-saving technologies of industrial capitalism, and thereby worked less than their preindustrial counterparts, access to new technologies in and of itself did not necessarily reduce these women's workloads. The vacuum cleaner, used by wealthier women in the 1920s and more widely available by the 1950s, is emblematic of this apparent paradox as the vacuum in theory ought to have allowed its users to more efficiently clean rugs and carpets. Yet vacuum cleaners in practice, as Ruth Cowan (1983) describes, resulted in women carrying and using heavy and cumbersome devices by themselves, whereas in preindustrial homes the moving, beating, and cleaning of rugs would have been less frequent and would have enlisted help from husbands and children now spending their time away from the home.

While capitalist society, which sent husbands to the factory and children first to the factory and then to school, often isolated women by erasing old ways of life, this alienation soon became an opportunity for profit. By the early 1900s, advertisements, frequently directed toward women, had evolved from mere product descriptions to strategies, crafted with the aid of psychological consultants, "to manipulate the consumer and associate images of physical, psychic, and social well-being with the acquisition of products" (Goodwin, Ackerman, and Kiron 1997, 143).[8]

Perhaps most prominently, a growing number of urban department stores enabled bourgeois women "to define themselves amid the anonymity of urban life" (Goodwin, Ackerman, and Kiron 1997, 139) and provided them with a respite from their household toil and frustrations. "'[T]he first public places—other than churches or cathedrals—which were considered respectable for (women) to visit without a male companion'" (Fiske 2000, 313),[9] department stores allowed the women who could afford to do so to shop, eat, and socialize in nearly all-women, glamorous, and status-boosting settings while fulfilling their new duties to be knowledgeable and well-provisioned homemakers. It was within the early department stores that "buying" became a recreational activity unto itself: "shopping." And it was here that "images transformed commodities into desirable items," even if "the aura of luxury in which the goods were presented compensated for their actual cheapness" (Goodwin, Ackerman, and Kiron 1997, 139). Notably, department stores did not address women's alienation and oppression at their roots so much as provided pleasure through shopping, an activity that simultaneously increased sexist stereotypes of women as "unproductive" and prodigal burdens who squandered men's hard-earned income. That such shopping was simultaneously predicated on the cheap labor of department stores' women employees additionally demonstrates the ways in which the profitable amelioration of capitalist alienation and exploitation can in fact reinforce these ills' material preconditions.

SAVING CAPITALISM FROM ITSELF (AGAIN)

While consumer society had become entrenched by the 1920s, it was ironically during the Depression of the 1930s that labor's long-running wages-versus-leisure debate was finally settled in favor of the former. Labor leaders had previously elected to promote higher wages over increased leisure with the justification that the "American standard of living" would, for those who qualified, produce a substantially improved quality of life (Glickman 1999). Yet, for rank and file members as well as other workers who were still unpersuaded that higher wages were preferable to greater leisure, the crisis years of the 1930s resolved the debate once and for all. For it was during the Depression that capitalism's contradictions became manifest in all of their absurdity. Mass overproduction produced severe deflation amid 25 percent unemployment. The bitterness of the unemployed, who could not afford commodities that collected dust on store shelves and who spent their days waiting in food relief lines while vainly hoping for work, made a mockery of the goal of increased leisure time as leisure was all most people had (Goodwin, Ackerman, and Kiron 1997, 43–45).[10] It was not just labor leaders now but a growing number of workers in general who observed that leisure under capitalism made little sense without the wages required to access goods.

The Keynesian response to the Depression radically reconfigured the state and identified the consumer as the center of the economy. Bolstering consumer demand in order to ease the crisis of overproduction, the New Deal put money into the pockets of consumers and instituted consumer protections in, among other areas, banking, pricing laws, and purity labeling. Expanding the precedent established a generation earlier during the Progressive Era, when the Federal Trade Commission Act, Meat Inspection Act, and Pure Food and Drug Act became law, New Deal policies demonstrated government's recognition that, left to their own devices, consumers would be fleeced into oblivion by a free market that was paradoxically dependent on them, and that a powerful external force was necessary to protect consumers and thereby stabilize capitalism.

Lest one conclude, however, that the new consumer protections reflected emerging consumer sovereignty, it is important to recall the significant government demands imposed on consumers when government saw fit. Keynesianism aside, the Depression only ended with the massive military spending accompanying the Second World War. Generating enough demand to absorb the glut in industrial production, the government accomplished what public projects and private consumers could not. As the government instituted its wartime command economy, it imposed severe restrictions on consumers. Amid the patriotic fervor of war, consumers not only purchased war bonds and stamps but also rationed, recycled, and salvaged goods and were encouraged to reconceptualize the roles and duties of consumers altogether. Indeed, nearly two hundred thousand people joined the Office of Price Administration and Civilian Supply (OPA), "citizen volunteers" who distributed ration books and investigated violations. Lizabeth Cohen (2003, 67) writes:

> In Syracuse, as across the nation, Americans learned that one of the chief ways to support the war on the home front was as responsible consumers. New rituals of patriotic citizenship evolved—obeying OPA price, rent, and rationing regulations and reporting violators; participating in recycling, scrap, and waste fat drives; planting Victory Gardens and "putting up" the harvest—all enforced through pacts of allegiance such as "The Consumer's Pledge for Total Defense" and the "Ten Commandments for Consumers." Suddenly tasks that had been viewed as private and domestic were brought into the civic arena and granted new political importance.

Yet, the very consumers who were encouraged and sometimes forced to save, ration, and sacrifice in the name of the war effort were enthusiastically encouraged to do the exact opposite once the war was over. With the reconversion to a peacetime economy, consumers' pent-up demand and savings were released in an unprecedented burst of sustained spending. However, attributing the new—in degree and kind—spending to the mere demand of consumers overlooks the ways in which government and business fundamentally restructured the economy and society in order to enable, direct, and shape this demand. Concerned about the prospects of a new depression following the war, the FDR and Truman administrations instituted laws and policies that encouraged consumers to not merely spend more but also to redesign their lives in ways that enabled consumption to be their dominant and defining activity. And as in other cases during the evolution of the consumer, consumers who "got ahead" were defined in part by those who were left behind.

Perhaps most famously, the G.I. Bill enabled millions of veterans to attend college, start businesses, and purchase homes via zero down, low interest, government-backed loans. Notably, preferences were granted to new construction over existing homes, encouraging a mass—and predominantly white—exodus from the cities to the suburbs, a massive demographic transformation further subsidized by the government's construction of roads and, in the 1950s, the Interstate Highway System.

While discussions of suburbanization frequently focus on the negative desire of whites to flee urban areas increasingly populated by people of color, suburbanization was initially influenced not only by "white flight" but also by the affirmative desire for the related but distinct return to the "country roots" (Jackson 1985) of preindustrial society.[11] That is, the migration to the suburbs reflected a mass rejection—for those who could afford it—of the alienation of urban living.

Whereas previous generations' need for accessible work bound people to the cities, the car allowed suburbanites to reside in the periphery and commute to work in the center. There is then an irony in the fact that the intended return to "country roots" precluded a return to "country work" and its associated independence and purposiveness. In spite of the wishes of those seeking simpler and better lives, the Jeffersonian ideal of country living had been denuded of its defining element. All that ultimately remained for busy commuters living within the architectural and cultural homogeneity of the suburbs was consumption.

If it was the state that helped launch and subsidize suburbanization, the market soon exploited what was to become a fundamentally reconfigured mode of living. The first step in moving to the suburbs entailed replacing often small urban dwellings with spacious—if uniform—homes with yards and often pools. Suburbanites' increased space then called to be filled with new commodities, triggering a perpetual process of acquisition unabashedly supported by the dominant culture amid competitive pressure to not fall behind neighbors in order to maintain a sense of social worth. At the same time, consumption in this era increasingly constituted what Zygmunt Bauman has described as a "pleasure-giving task" that migrated from the fulfillment of finite *need* to the attempted fulfillment of infinite *desire* without, unlike in the early department stores, any justification of utility (Bauman 2004).

New suburbanites who nevertheless needed to shop were initially inconvenienced by having to either commute downtown or rely on the still limited shops of their local town centers (Cohen 2003, 257). But by the late 1950s, a new commercial structure had developed in the form of the regional shopping center. The shopping centers enabled sellers to avoid the costs of conducting business both within the cities, which were increasingly marked by traffic and limited parking, and the undeveloped land of the smaller towns (Cohen 2003, 258). Although malls would later appear in the cities, merchants initially embraced the suburbs as a "unique opportunity to reinvent community life with their private projects at its heart" (Cohen 2003, 258). Promising to meet customers' needs for shopping and community, the new shopping centers represented, according to Cohen, the "'new city' of the postwar era, a community center suited to an economy and society built around mass consumption" (2003, 259).

While the shopping centers resembled the department stores before them in that both catered to the economic and social needs of socially isolated customers, the shopping centers represented a quantitative and qualitative expansion of scale. "'Bringing the market to the people instead of people to the market'" (Cohen 2003, 261), the centers commercialized vast areas of public space now aesthetically standardized and politically centralized under the control of private management (263). And whereas the department stores ameliorated the alienation predominantly of upper-class and middle-class urban women, whose primary connection to the commercial world had been radio, shopping centers offered meaning and ritual to women, men, and children whose primary connection to the commercial world was the more powerful and arresting medium of television. Filling a void created by modern, now suburban, life, the mall—which, with its "balance, symmetry, and order," George Ritzer likens to the religious centers of ancient civilizations—employed capitalist spectacles to "enchant" a world that had been stripped of its mystery, magic, and excitement (Ritzer 2010, 7).

Of course a fundamental difference between malls and the earlier religious centers is that malls provided recreation, ritual, and meaning in a thoroughly commercial setting. Expressing an "emphatic denial of the virtue of procrastination," consumerism increasingly centered on "the blissful instant of acquisition" (and related disposal), making *possession* a mere, and often anticlimactic, means to an end (Bauman 2004). We should additionally be unsurprised that opportunities to engage in such communal activity, again, excluded large sections of society who were deemed "undesirable." Developers and merchants of the "new city" aimed to keep out "unwanted urban elements, such as vagrants, prostitutes, disruptive rebels, racial minorities, and poor people" (Cohen 2003, 265). Bus routes to some centers were designed to serve suburban women at the expense of low-income urban residents who were disproportionately people of color. Notably, it was only after formal segregationist barriers fell in the mid-1960s that the suburbs began to lose their luster as putative havens from urban blight, and today the suburbs are littered with "dead malls," "largely vacant shells" that have lost their ability to generate adequate profit and have thus been deprived of their value within capitalism (Hudson and O'Connell 2009). At the same time, much of what made malls captivating is now nearly extinct (for instance, brick and mortar record and book stores) or else has transformed and migrated to individual homes for private use (for instance, movie theaters and video arcades). That is, the amelioration of alienation by malls had always been only incidental to their ability to manufacture profit. And while it is tempting to account for such transformations by asserting that "this is what consumers want," it is important to note that the effective importation of the mall into the home is less connected to consumers' pursuit of pleasure than to what is—amid the shrinkage of leisure time—euphemistically referred to as "convenience."

By the 1970s, as industrialization began to give way to the growing financial and service sectors, whites began returning to cities whose depressed real estate provided ample investment and rental opportunities, not to mention more excitement than the culturally arid and alienating suburbs—although such excitement (including the pursuit of sex and romance) was ultimately to become, as in the suburbs, substantially mediated by the Internet, without which residents of even the liveliest cities would be relegated to enormous impracticalities if not effective hermitage. The ensuing gentrification of the cities in effect repeated the cycle of suburbanization in reverse. Predominantly white consumers helped initiate both processes, and numerous people of color who in the first phase had been abandoned in underfunded and dangerous cities were in the second phase priced out of their homes and forced to relocate to the increasingly abandoned peripheries.

The extended but arguably unified history of suburbanization and gentrification demonstrates not only the generally competitive and particularly racialized character of consumption under U.S. capitalism but also how transformations in the productive sphere prompt and structure new consumption patterns and lifestyles. Upwardly mobile, predominantly white veterans moved to the suburbs during the heyday of the U.S. industrial economy following the Second World War. The explosion of consumer spending introduced new demands for greater physical space for consumption. Suburbanization corresponded to a shift in the political economy wherein consumers' greater access to and reliance on large durable goods, most importantly cars, both enabled (via commuting) and required accommodation in large houses outside of the cities (Cohen 2003, chapter 5). Conversely, the gentrification that began several decades later followed a new shift in a now deindustrializing economy that increasingly emphasized immaterial labor. The finance and service economies tended to generate smaller commodities culminating in the tech industry's production of laptops and smartphones with which people can conduct their professional and social lives and which can house libraries, record collections, encyclopedias, personal calendars, and cameras while easily fitting inside of the smallest urban studio. Just as social status today frequently accrues to upper-middle-class consumers who can afford to "declutter" and "minimize" their frequently smaller homes, the working classes are frowned upon for driving large cars and frequenting box stores such as Walmart where they purchase cheap outsized furniture and entertainment systems (Land 2016). This historic role reversal of consumption patterns demonstrates not only the decisive influence that production plays in determining consumption trends but also that the status attending wealthier and white consumption often has no intrinsic relationship to the objective character of what is being consumed and is, instead, fundamentally relational (Veblen 1994 [1899]; Holt 2000; Bourdieu 1984; Warner, Meeker, and Eells 1949; Simmel 1957 [1904]).

WORKING HARD AND HARDLY WORKING: THE CONSUMER 2.0

The new commercial landscape of daily life did not merely offer exclusionary ritual and meaning to relatively privileged consumers in the name of profit extraction. It also made demands. While in early consumer society, as discussed above, consumers had to learn how to consume and frequently occupied a relatively passive role within commercial processes initiated and largely structured by producers and merchants, consumers in the postwar era frequently performed proactive work in the process of production itself. To be sure, consumers were still acted upon and influenced by increasingly sophisticated advertising and spatial-control strategies. Fast-food restaurants such as McDonald's, for instance, use hard, uncomfortable chairs and tacky colors to discourage customers from staying too long, while Las Vegas hotels feature mirror-filled, labyrinthine casinos designed to trap, often intoxicated, customers in the casinos for as long as possible. Yet consumers had also become mature—or trained—enough that they could be delegated, often tacitly, tasks by business, from self-service, to gas-pumping, to furniture-building, to recycling, to using ATMs (Ritzer 2004; Illich 1981; Lambert 2015).

McDonald's provides a particularly prominent illustration of some of the ways in which business had trained customers to participate in the production process. The restaurant's very design—from the placement of its entrances to its garbage cans—prompts customers what to do and where to do it, from standing in line to quickly ordering and paying to taking their food to their tables, bussing them, and discarding their waste (Leidner 1993). Similarly, the drive-thru trains customers to efficiently take their places within and move along what is in effect a customer assembly line. In a joke recounted by Robin Leidner (1993, 45), a customer who would enter a McDonald's and ask "'So, what's good today?'" would provoke the contempt of others not only for slowing down the production process but also for being so abjectly ignorant of the capitalist-generated norms of consumer society.

The enormous retailer Walmart, albeit in a different manner than that of the Southern California-based fast-food chain, also helped revolutionize the ways that business makes demands on customers. Sam Walton's store originated in rural Arkansas and targeted as its clientele working-class and poor customers, often farmers—or their children—who had been foreclosed during the Depression (Lichtenstein 2009). The Ozarks had been one of the country's poorest regions during the time of Walmart's rise, and the retailer skillfully reduced costs in the distribution chain as well as through, among other strategies, customer self-service. Customers not only learned to navigate the stores' massive warehouses with limited help from employees but also frequently drove substantial distances to reach freestanding Walmart stores that avoided the high rents of operating out of the more accessible malls. While Walmart has been lauded for its inexpensive products, its cost-cutting has also been achieved, as has been often noted, through the use of highly exploited Chinese labor and aggressive antiunionism inside the United States.[12] In a similar vein, the emergence of just-in-time production in a variety of industries undoubtedly reduced consumers' wait time for products but did so primarily at the expense of intensifying the precariousness of workers who could no longer depend on consistent employment.

Since the early 1970s, as the postwar boom came to an end and the value of labor began to decline, U.S. society has been increasingly instructed that people's real worth lies in the realm of consumption, representing a return to the explicit values of the "consumerist turn" of the early 1900s (Glickman 1999). However, in contrast to the older industrial economy, the burgeoning service economy eliminated the physical separation between workers and consumers that had characterized manufacturing. The "good life" promised to the new "sovereign consumer" was less based on access to factory-produced goods than on entitlement to the "emotional labor" of service workers who have been trained to work not only with their hands and minds but also with their smiles, feelings, and personalities (Hochschild 2003 [1983]; Leidner 1993). What was generally left unsaid was that it was increasingly the consumer who was expected to monitor and discipline those providing this labor.

As the service sector grew it increasingly solicited customer feedback. "How are we doing?" signs and stickers became commonplace as did restaurant and hotel questionnaires that asked customers to provide feedback on their experiences, specifically regarding their encounters with employees (Fuller and Smith 1991). This form of customer work has exponentially expanded with the growth of the Internet and its countless websites in which users are encouraged—often in the name of communal duty—to detail their experiences with everything from plumbers to teachers to doctors to restaurants to the innumerable products sold on mega-websites such as Amazon. Whereas pre-Internet customers would have had to go out of their way to complete and deposit a "How are we doing?" card after a meal, websites such as Yelp have incorporated customer feedback into the routines of our daily lives.[13]

While the Internet certainly did not create consumer management, the personal involvement and intensiveness of consumer management, and prosumption in general, are particularly conducive to that medium. Previously, radio and television's unilaterality paralleled the needs of advertisers who sought silent and passive audiences to absorb their messages. Yet, radio listeners and TV viewers did become "active," criticizing programs, becoming wise to advertisers' tactics, and at times boycotting products, all of which pushed advertisers to develop ever more creative techniques for influencing increasingly savvy consumers (Newman 2004). Contemporary prosumption emerged in this context not only as a cost-cutting measure but also as a means for allowing companies to reach sophisticated and rebellious consumers by recruiting them into the production process itself, where their creative energies and criticality could be channeled toward profit making (Zwick, Bonsu, and Darmody 2008; Gladwell 1997).

Indeed, the Internet was the ideal medium for consumer work insofar as it provided the "mechanism of reply" (Adorno and Horkheimer 2002 [1944], 96; Zwick, Bonsu, and Darmody 2008) prior media lacked and thereby enabled far more interactive, intimate, and personally meaningful social exchanges and work. The Internet's inherent interactivity provides its users with a control that is concomitantly predicated on the control of users' spatial movements and thoughts. Indeed, the physical immediacy required by a computer keyboard and screen or smartphone is indicative of the degree to which the Internet commands, and captivates, users' entire attention. Radio enabled listeners to move about freely and even mentally tune out its sounds if they chose. TV's visual stimulation proved far more fixating than radio's audio, giving rise to the notorious couch potato, but TV's unilateral dissemination nonetheless did not require the level of intellectual engagement of an Internet user who, for instance, *writes* a comment or review and argues, jokes, and flirts with other people online. Internet use is, in general, a distinctly totalizing experience that is proportionate to the intellectual effort required for much contemporary prosumption. This hardly means that there is an absence of critical self-awareness or rebellion online, just that it is increasingly difficult for such subversion to escape recuperation.

The Internet's form structures its content in another way. The characteristic instantaneity and immediacy of the Internet encourages, it has been argued, a tunnel-vision detrimental to both reflection and perspective. As Paul Virilio observes, "The faster we go, the more we look ahead in anticipation and lose our lateral vision. Screens are like windshields in a car: with increased speed, we lose the sense of lateralization, which is an infirmity in our being in the world, its richness, its relief, its depth of field" (Virilio 2012, 36–37). The Internet then, amplifying existing societal tendencies, tends to reward speed and visibility over content. This helps explain the practice in which some commenters celebrate being "first" to respond to an article irrespective of the content of any other comments they want to make, as well as the prevalence of angry miscommunications and flame wars that sometimes mar even seemingly innocuous online exchanges. Beyond such effects, the Internet's instantaneousness accelerates a form of consumption which is not only characterized first and foremost by acquisition for acquisition's sake but also in which, as Bauman has observed, *the distance between* acquisition and disposal has exponentially narrowed (Bauman 2004). One need only think of the ways in which products are often purchased on Amazon or eBay. Relatedly, the fact that Facebook "likes" are not owned or kept but rather immediately "consumed" helps explain the often frantic compulsiveness with which they are pursued. The pleasure, literally endorphins, they provide is concomitant to the brevity with which they retain their value amid an online sea of perpetually shifting content. The Internet provides the ideal platform for and distillation of contemporary consumption: pure acquisition.

To be sure, the Internet did not initially enable substantial profit beyond the wild speculation of dot-com booms. On the contrary, as Robert McChesney (2013) has shown, in the early days of the Internet media corporations were deeply concerned that they would be unable to sell advertising space—or produce profit in general—on a medium that had apparently put an end to information scarcity. Following the passage of the 1996 Telecommunications Bill, media corporations increasingly monopolized the Internet and attempted, often unsuccessfully, to monetize websites, whether through cookies-based targeted advertising, paywalls and other "walled gardens" that require payment for entry, or the dramatic expansion of copyright protections (McChesney 2013). Yet it was not until the advent of Web 2.0—most prominently Facebook—that it became apparent what the profit-producing potential of the Internet would look like.

Although it is tempting to dismiss it as "timeless" or "natural," the energetic and what we might call actualized consumer of today did not simply and inevitably appear as an effect of the Internet but is instead the product of specific historic institutional developments, not least in the realm of production. Paul Du Gay and Graeme Salaman delineate several key social and economic transformations that helped pave the way for this form of intellectual, consumer-rights oriented, prosumption (Du Gay and Salaman 1992).

Specifically, they note that the crisis of the Keynesian welfare state in the 1970s and 1980s, along with a shift from the "passive, easily pleased" (617) consumer of the Fordist era to the demanding, knowledgeable, and differentiated consumer of the modern era, introduced new opportunities for, and demands on, business. Business frequently responded by replacing the traditional model of vertical organization and hierarchical administrative control with a new strategy revolving around the so-called sovereign customer. In particular, many companies began to organize their work structures and practices around what Du Gay and Salaman refer to as a "customer-supplier" relationship, which imposes market logic on the internal workings of business departments themselves. For instance, employees were now encouraged to treat one another not as coworkers but as "customers" who needed to be pleased, while, under the guise of "customer sovereignty," employees were encouraged to treat actual customers as "managers" whose needs must be prioritized above all. While Du Gay and Salaman note that this notion of "customer sovereignty" is in fact exaggerated, the internal operational changes that businesses have implemented under its name are real. It was within this context of business's deliberate and self-interested elevation of the concept of "customer sovereignty" that the service industry began to increasingly incorporate customers into the management of service workers. Echoing Fuller and Smith, Du Gay and Salaman argue that using customers to manage service workers enables a far more flexible and effective means to ensure, for instance, that employees maintain the desired ". . . facial expression, nuances of verbal tone, or type of eye-contact" (621), subtle interpersonal behaviors difficult to govern by managerial policy.

Simultaneously, an expanding "culture of enterprise" encouraged the consumer, like the employee, to view himself or herself

> as an individual in search of meaning and fulfilment, looking to "add value" in every sphere of existence. Paid work and consumption are just different playing grounds for the same activity; different terrains upon which the enterprising self seeks to master, fulfil and better itself. In making oneself a better sovereign consumer, or a better employee, one becomes a more virtuous and empowered human being (1992, 627).

The penetration of this notion of the "enterprising self" into the public and private spheres deeply resonated with innumerable people who increasingly conceived of their lives as an "enterprise of self," and whose idea and pursuit of personal improvement was fundamentally structured by market relations themselves. It is within this context—a post-Keynesian, or neoliberal, era permeated with competitive individualism fostered not only by schooling, work, sports, and entertainment but also by a robust "self-help" industry—that consumers came to provide to businesses not only their most creative and personal works but also unpaid feedback on employees in the name of a virtuous, ethical, and empowering worldview.

The online prosumer represents the culmination of the twentieth-century consumer. Originally treated as passive and directed through advertising, branding, and packaging as well as national campaigns and cultural pressures, consumers have become savvy and ideologically indoctrinated enough to be "freed" (Zwick, Bonsu, and Darmody 2008) from overt capitalist control. This has enabled them to perform far more independent, intellectual, and creative work through a technology that provides the "mechanism of reply" that had historically been denied to consumers of radio and television. This freeing was predicated not only on the maturation of consumer subjects and the mass availability of the Internet but also on the market's growing domination of all areas of life. Thus, ads no longer have to instruct consumers to buy particular products but can instead communicate brands' "auras," and it is mere knowledge of the latter that equips consumers to independently find or, more meaningfully, "discover" the desired commodities. Describing the marketing strategy of producer-consumer "co-creation," Zwick, Bonsu, and Darmody (2008, 177) write, "It is a form of government of consumers that gives birth to an active consumer whose independent, creative, and voluntary activities can now effectively be channeled into raw material for the firm's commodity production." Drawing consumers into the innovation and production of products, business has not only tapped into the creative resources and competitive drive of consumers—expropriating vast sources of creative, intellectual, and civic energy that had hitherto existed outside the market—but in doing so has incorporated sometimes defiant and cynical consumers as personally invested (though unpaid) stakeholders in both particular enterprises and capitalism itself (Zwick, Bonsu, and Darmody 2008). For instance, business has recruited all manner of consumers to participate in (unpaid) design contests (for example, for potato chips, teddy bears, and Lifesavers) and "DIY" sites in which prosumers customize their own products, paying money for the right to create designs whose rights are then controlled by business owners (Zwick, Bonsu, and Darmody 2008, 181–84).

The Internet has also facilitated the dramatic expansion of the related practice of reader feedback on news, sports, entertainment, and other articles. It is not uncommon for commenters to note that they clicked on an article specifically in order to read the comments, which, to be sure, are often witty, informed, and entertaining, and which can be viewed as instant polls measuring readers' opinions. Internet users additionally spend countless hours writing blogs, creating and maintaining profiles on networking sites such as Facebook and LinkedIn and dating sites such as OKCupid, and producing and uploading videos on sites such as YouTube or photos on Instagram. Among the many motivations driving these users is the competitive drive to stand out and win acclaim (or "likes") for their contributions. Indeed, without such individual competitiveness—which, regardless of its putative universality, is reified and amplified under capitalism—and the desire to distinguish ourselves from mass anonymous society, prosumption in its current form would arguably not exist.

This freeing of the consumer, it should be noted, can be compared to but should not be conflated with the freeing of labor that, Marx observed, constituted a core precondition for the emergence of capitalism. With the end of feudalism, peasants were severed from the land and, with it, their ability to self-subsist. Freedom meant that people were thrown into a world in which they were free to (attempt to) sell their labor power to owners of private property, which workers are both excluded from and dependent on in order to earn wages. This freeing—in which labor was released from the obligations (and protections) of a generally rigid and oppressive feudal hierarchy—was established with and maintained by mass institutional violence. By contrast, prosumers have not been freed from capitalist relations but from a different, more primitive and externally costly, form of capitalist consumption. Less a revolutionary transformation than a quantitative-cum-qualitative intensification of existing relations, the freeing of modern consumers has not been based on direct external coercion but has instead relied on the mass internalization of consumerist ideology.

For, as Zwick, Bonsu, and Darmody (2008, 165) note, capitalists' increased control over consumers does not entail domination. On the contrary:

> Customer management, then, as the exertion of political power to produce particular forms of life, clearly does not mean domination because marketers presuppose, and in fact expect, the consumer subject to act, innovate, tinker and run free. The marketing challenge posed by the co-creation model rests, of course, with establishing ambiences that program consumer freedom to evolve in ways that permit the harnessing of consumers' newly liberated, productive capabilities.

Large numbers of consumers have specifically "run free" to consumer review sites. As we will see, on these sites consumers have cultivated communities of like-minded reviewers who often exhibit an honesty, fairness, and conscientiousness that evince a shared sense of communal "duty" and solidarity. Writing for "fun," pleasure, and status but also from a sense of social obligation to "pay it forward," these users enact a shared "code" that would seem to defy the individualist orientation of the consumer. Online customer reviewers have created a new community—albeit a largely virtual one. This is a community in which members work, have obligations, and are held to account. But it is also one that produces profit through increased site traffic and advertising revenue that users do not partake in. And it is one in which the consumer reviews that are the fruits of the community's labor are frequently used to dominate wage workers, whom we might refer to as the online consumer manager's displaced external antagonist or Other. That is, insofar as online consumer managers are cooperative, it is cooperation born of a competition against individual businesses (versus, say, business as such) that in practice primarily harms workers and, insofar as most consumers are workers as well, thereby ultimately online consumer managers themselves.

While it is tempting to describe the evolution of prosumption as beginning with the menial work of "McDonaldization" and culminating with the intellectual labor of commodity development and innovation (Zwick, Bonsu, and Darmody 2008), I am arguing that prosumption has reached a new stage of depth, power, and potential profitability—or control—through the practice of online customer management. For it is through online customer management that consumers channel their sense of social duty and desire for community not merely to develop and innovate commodities for businesses but to manage businesses' employees. In the future, customer management could facilitate the reduction of non-profit producing workers in the form of professional management and therefore presents enormous potential for capitalists. In the here and now, however, customer management reveals the ever increasing extent to which capitalism has made and remade human beings in its own image.

THE EXPLOITATION OF ALIENATION

What then does it mean to describe prosumption, and with it online consumer management, as exploitation? At first glance it seems counterintuitive to characterize these activities as exploitative, since, as P. J. Rey observes (2012, 400), Marx's descriptions of labor exploitation focused on the "'cattle-like conditions'" of factory work during the Industrial Revolution, in which workers were coerced through market mechanisms to work under the threat of starvation. By contrast, prosumption—Rey examines Facebook as its "paradigmatic example"—is voluntary and frequently pleasurable. Prosumers do not have managers and only create what they choose to. According to Rey, however, in technical terms prosumerism is in fact exploitative insofar as prosumption generates wealth that its users, even if they are not waged employees, do not partake in.[14]

Yet Rey argues that exploitation—beyond the absence of brutal factory conditions—is qualitatively different under prosumption. Specifically, because prosumers perform immaterial labor and are presumably not confronted with material scarcity, under prosumption use value and exchange value are no longer mutually exclusive. That is, while one could not simultaneously sell and use an umbrella, the production of massive immaterial digital labor allows prosumers to both exchange their work (e.g., with the website owner, who is interested in selling advertising space) and still use it for their own purposes. Notwithstanding his caveat that immaterial labor is challenging to quantify, Rey argues that the more useful the prosumption is to the prosumer, the less exploitative it is.

However, it is important that such notions of usefulness be problematized given that prosumption is often devoted not only to the shadow work of daily existence in capitalism but also to the technically voluntary but functionally coerced activity of, for instance, generating and maintaining professional online profiles on websites such as LinkedIn. Not having a Facebook account can in fact make workers seem "suspicious" to potential employers (White 2012). While efforts must be made to maintain one's marketability in capitalism, it is through prosumption that these efforts become effectively mandatory and, relatedly, monetized. That is, usefulness and exploitation need not be mutually exclusive. Indeed, website owners profit off of prosumers' unpaid work regardless of whether prosumers find it useful.

It is additionally significant that because prosumption is formally unwaged it generally cannot, for Marx if not Rey, create the surplus value and thereby capitalist growth that can only be generated through the exploitation of waged labor. That is, for Marx prosumption in itself would by definition not constitute exploitation. Instead of resolving the problem of declining economic growth, prosumption can in fact exacerbate capitalist crises insofar as it replaces waged workers with unwaged ones.

Paradoxically, prosumers *can* increase individual website's revenue by contributing content, which in turn attracts more visitors and enables platform owners to demand higher rates from advertisers. Prosumers additionally enhance the value of websites through providing their own personal data, which Nick Srnicek likens to raw material that can be extracted and refined, to website owners. As Srnicek notes, "Unlike in manufacturing, in platforms competitiveness is not judged solely by the criterion of a maximal difference between costs and prices; data collection and analysis also contribute to how competitiveness is judged and ranked," leading to ever more intensive extraction and analysis of users' personal information (Srnicek 2017, 97). It is this drive for data that, for instance, helps explain the emergence of the so-called Internet of Things, an effect less of consumer demand than of the interests of capital (Srnicek 2017, 100). Srnicek convincingly observes that while "the more numerous the users who interact on a platform, the more valuable the entire platform becomes for each one of them" this influx of overall supply—whether in content or personal data—need *not* produce a decline in demand and prices insofar as Web 2.0 is highly monopolistic (Srnicek 2017, 97). Just the same, because users' unpaid contributions to websites do not formally constitute wage labor, such activity in itself cannot generate surplus value, and the general crisis in economic growth—in spite of and in part due to all this frenetic activity—continues unabated.

In some ways, however, prosumption does resemble exploited "living labor" insofar as it is part of an *ongoing* exchange (versus, for instance, a machine, or slave, whose labor value has already been added to it and is thus constituted as "dead labor") that produces the value of a particular commodity. Facebook, YouTube, and other Web 2.0 sites are as profitable as they are in large part due to the millions of users that participate on them. Yet it is not the mere fact that users generate wealth that they do not partake in that characterizes prosumption as exploitative as Marx used the term. Prosumption in itself can be thought of as exploitative but only if we assume that users produce wealth that outstrips the value of *a wage* that they do in fact receive, albeit a virtual wage that, as with monetary wages, can never be sufficient to eliminate the want that leads prosumers/workers to pursue it in the first place. While such activity does not constitute, as Marx described it, wage labor per se (such a virtual wage is neither based on a universal equivalent nor is it exchangeable in perpetuity), the compulsive manner in which, say, prosumers produce content for websites in order to endlessly acquire ephemeral "likes" expresses what we might call *virtual wage* labor.

Yet there is a form of prosumption that in fact increases the exploitation of *actual* wage laborers and thereby does help generate surplus value: online consumer management. For here prosumers interact with, directly or indirectly, workers. Through monitoring and reporting on employees, online consumer managers have heightened workers' anxiety and increased their productivity. While it is undoubtedly difficult to quantify such increases in productivity, we can nevertheless observe instances in which it is occurring, recognize the incentives that capitalist governance has in fostering such activity, and identify the potential such activity has for transforming leisure, work, and management in the future. But before doing so, let us examine one more core feature of prosumption: alienation.

While conceding that it is indeed difficult for prosumption to consistently minimize exploitation, Rey (2012, 401) does in fact argue that prosumption can dramatically reduce alienation, which, following Marx, he defines as "the process through which capitalism disrupts workers' natural relationships to the objects they create, their labor, their species-being, and to other people." With the division between production and consumption largely eliminated, and with prosumers' material needs met, prosumption allows for the spontaneous and intentional activity that defines humanity's "'species-being.'" In fact, Rey suggests (2012, 410) that contemporary capitalism has an active interest in reducing alienation: "Capitalism in the digital age does not merely diminish the need for mindless, coerced labor but actually reconfigures itself to promote and benefit from intentional, spontaneous activity (i.e., unalienated labor). Rather than inhibiting such activity, capitalists have learned to extract new forms of value from it."

Yet there is a second form of alienation that Rey does not address: alienation from the means of production, a material alienation related to but distinct from psychological alienation (Marx 1994 [1844]; Chitty 2014). Prosumption can very well minimize the first, sociological, form of alienation. Simultaneously, it actively reproduces material alienation insofar as prosumers do not own the sites—or means of production—that they contribute to. As Edward Comor (2010, 450) writes:

> The seemingly free and autonomous prosumer has not, however, forsaken predominant structures and relations, for how could she if private property and contract relations remain entrenched institutions, both online and off. Moreover, the prosumer's dependency on the corporations that own, design and run the essential infrastructures through which people work and consume leaves little room for genuinely autonomous development.

Accordingly, prosumers react to various site directives and cues that formally or informally help structure prosumers' content, and site redesigns require prosumers to periodically reorient themselves in order to continue participating on the site, a sometimes frustrating task underscoring the separation between the decisions of site owners and the prosumers who must conform to those decisions. Facebook not only encourages its users to post pictures but ensures that these pictures conform to various rules, banning, for instance, certain violent images as well as images of breastfeeding women. A photo posted on Facebook then—beyond being freely licensed to that site which can then do with it what it wishes—becomes in effect a "Facebook photo," a self-perpetuating product that can inspire and simultaneously structure further innovation and activity. That is, prosumption assuredly mediates between capitalists and consumers, but, insofar as prosumers are excluded from the rights of property ownership, it is a mediation reflecting fundamentally disparate power relations.

Notably, Facebook was recently considering enabling users to install virtual tip jars onto their pages,[15] allowing users to make donations to fellow users who they enjoy and support (Newton 2016). This potential monetization at first glance resembles restaurant tipping, in which customers subsidize employers' labor costs by tipping servers in putative exchange for "good service." However, insofar as Facebook users are not customers but instead provide the site with their unpaid labor, Facebook is proposing a system in which prosumers would be encouraged to not only *produce* Facebook's content but also *pay for* content produced by fellow prosumers (and likely hope to earn their own tips as well). Given the hierarchical and competitive social organization of Facebook—reflecting that of capitalist society itself—in which not everyone, by definition, can be popular, there are bound to be increasingly more tippers than tippees, with the latter invariably shrinking through competition with one another for greater shares of the former (Dean

2013). This potential pay-to-work (or pay-to-prosume) setup not only reflects the material alienation characterizing prosumption but also suggests some of the ways in which prosumption's reduction of sociological alienation amid the perpetuation of material alienation is problematic.

The sociological alienation that helps inspire people to prosume is inseparable from capitalism's historic destruction of subsistence communities and extended families and its ensuing establishment of industrial and postindustrial urban societies. Capitalism as a social system has not only been highly individualizing but also is in itself highly ephemeral. It is a perpetual struggle for many individuals to find their moorings in a system in which "all that is solid melts into air." Although capitalism has historically undermined existing forms of community it simultaneously gives (or sells) new forms of community in return, albeit communities that are in capitalism's image and reproduce its material roots. Therefore, insofar as being a Yelp reviewer can remedy users' sociological alienation through finding a group of like-minded online friends, contributing to Yelp, and thereby the market system itself, reproduces the material conditions of alienation that helped lead people to prosume on Yelp in the first place. Indeed, Comor (2010, 451) describes a contradiction at the heart of the relationship between prosumption and alienation:

> Directly or indirectly, most contemporary expressions of individualism and one's pursuit of social connection are taking place in ways that elaborate exchange value interests or capital's general reproduction. The individual therefore can be understood to be prosuming in response to his alienation while, in so doing, deepening this very condition.[16]

Prosumption can be seen as a displacement for unfulfilled desire, promising to alleviate alienation while reproducing its essential cause through enriching capitalist corporations and thereby reinforcing capitalism itself. On one hand, we need to acknowledge that prosumption, at least in the short-term, can provide happiness. Accusations of "false consciousness" are not only patronizing but also ultimately naïve. As Adorno made clear in his response to Veblen, "Even the commodity fetishist who has succumbed to conspicuous consumption to the point of obsession participates in the truth-content of happiness . . . (which) contain(s) the recognition of society, of the whole, as the true subject of happiness" (Adorno 1984 [1967], 87). On the other hand, the compulsive and insatiable lust for "likes," "retweets," "follows," "hearts" and the like, has no end point because the source, and ultimate unfulfillment, of the desire (for affirmation, approval, sociality, etc.) is being continually reproduced in the non-virtual world. Even on dating sites, which are ostensibly self-terminating for those seeking long-term relationships, users often complain of "serial dating," as they are commonly reluctant to commit to cultivating a relationship lest they miss out by not "keeping their options open" to finding ever more perfect matches from the seemingly endless cornucopia on display.

While Rey describes prosumption as spontaneous and intentional (that is, nonalienated), such immediacy is nevertheless structured by intrinsically competitive social conditions in which individuals' efforts are quantified through money or likes.[17] Nonalienated labor, for Marx, would have every reason to be cooperative, while prosumption is generally (and sometimes viciously) competitive. Even webpages ostensibly devoted to subversive art monitor site visits, suggesting the incommensurability between monetary-oriented quantification and radical and transformative thought. Replicating in the virtual world capitalism's definition and quantification of success, the potential monetization of Facebook pages indicates that prosumption has always been not only exploitative but also inherently capitalistic. Prosumption's reduction of alienation has been achieved not through the liberation of human beings but through capital's triumph over a human subjectivity that is increasingly devoted to and unified with the competitive and unending needs of profit.

NOTES

1. Gabriel and Lang (2015 [1995]) present a useful typology, concluding with "consumer as worker," of consumers' many roles.
2. This debate is skillfully recounted in editors Neva R. Goodwin, Frank Ackerman, and David Kiron's *The Consumer Society* (Washington, DC: Island Press, 1997)
3. John Kenneth Galbraith similarly refers to the "paramount position of production" under capitalism. *The Affluent Society*. Boston, MA: Houghton Mifflin, 1958.
4. The authors are here referring to the argument of James Beniger.
5. Daniel Boorstin quoted in Beniger.
6. John Fiske (2000) describes the sense of social control such semiotic wealth can provide in his discussion of teenage-swarmed Australian shopping malls.
7. Evan Watkins (1993) eloquently discusses the production of human obsolescence in consumer culture. See also Jean Baudrillard (1981).
8. Lest anyone assume that such descriptions are passé, it is useful to consider leaked documents showing that Facebook has boasted to advertisers that it can identify the emotional state of teenagers on the site and can even alert advertisers to '"moments when young people need a confidence boost"' (Twenge 2017).
9. Rachel Bowlby (1987) quoted in Fiske.
10. Goodwin, Ackerman, and Kiron are describing the argument of Gary Cross (1993).
11. Lewinnek (2014), examining early suburbanization in Chicago, emphasizes that anti-Black racism was embedded in suburbanization from the beginning, as highly diverse suburbanites sought to take advantage of "the mortgages of whiteness."
12. Nelson Lichtenstein has shown that the low wages/cheap goods tradeoff is an unequal one, as the type of consumer spending done at Walmart constitutes only one-fifth of total consumer spending. That is, consumers would be better off with higher wages (most of which are spent on rent, healthcare, and education) even if it meant higher prices at Walmart, which is not mentioning the shoddiness of the products frequently sold at its stores.
13. Insofar as so much of our lives indeed occur online.

14. Ritzer and Jurgenson (2010) also argue that online prosumption, even though part of the production system is turned over to prosumers (e.g., with Facebook pages) in a way that would not have existed in other forms of prosumption (e.g., McDonald's would not allow customers to grill their own burgers), is exploitative in that profits are kept by the company, a point made by others including Fuchs (2010; 2013). There are exceptions, however, such as popular YouTube prosumers who receive (often tiny) cuts of the advertising revenue their pages earn. Tapscott and Williams (2006), by contrast, argue that prosumption on Web 2.0 is not exploitative insofar as prosumers are part of a "culture of generosity," are able to connect with others and express themselves, and frequently receive public recognition for their unpaid contributions. It should additionally be noted that capitalism in the digital age is undoubtedly still based on exploitatively extracted material resources, such as columbite-tantalite, and effectively coerced labor in sweatshops and fields around the globe (Beller 2013).

15. Or, rather, Facebook's pages.

16. Comor cogently argues that the extent of alienation corresponds to the type of prosumer, with the mass majority of prosumers functioning as mere tools of capital. While there is in fact a highly specialized minority of prosumers who can potentially ameliorate their alienation through prosumption, Comor suggests that these privileged prosumers are unlikely to undermine their class interests through subversive prosumption.

17. I am not, to be sure, criticizing competition in some universalist sense but rather the forms it takes within the unequal and alienated context of capitalism. Even within capitalism, however, there are arguably positive forms of competition, but I argue that their frequent absence is a general characteristic of prosumption.

Chapter Three

Yelp

Working for Pleasure (and to Make Others Rich)

At any given moment, you can be fairly sure that someone is writing a review of a restaurant for the website Yelp.[1] This person is likely carefully crafting and editing this review with the aim of informing and possibly entertaining those who will read it. The writer is likely describing the food in detail, and odds are that the review also discusses the restaurant's service. Once finished and uploaded, this review will join a depository of over 155 million other reviews, which together constitute an enterprise valued at over three billion dollars and is used by approximately 100 million unique visitors per month (Yelp 2018). It is also highly likely that the restaurant manager will read this review and, if it serves management's interests, incorporate it into the management of the restaurant. That is, Yelp restaurant reviewers produce value in two distinct arenas. First, the massive website uses reviews to increase its traffic and thereby its advertising rates and revenue (in contrast to most Web 2.0 sites, Yelp does not sell user data). Second, Yelp reviewers have provided for free what restaurants often pay for: ubiquitous surveillance of and feedback on employees. While Yelp and restaurants have a decidedly ambivalent, and often antagonistic, relationship, restaurants have successfully used Yelp reviews to increase managerial control over and intensify the productivity of workers.[2]

It is notable that the Yelp that is widely known today is substantially different from its first incarnation. In 2004, the site was launched as in effect a community bulletin board on which users could exchange business referrals (O'Brien 2007). The site's owners discovered, however, that users were paying far more attention to a feature of the site that enabled users to write their own unsolicited reviews, and the following year a new version of the site, now centered around user-generated reviews, was successfully launched (O'Brien 2007). That is, in its very development, Yelp illustrates the ways in which contemporary consumers can, and do, make their voices heard, mediating production.

At the same time, the effects of Yelp reviews, specifically on workers, tells us much about the limits of consumer power. Specifically, reviewers' increasing ability to monitor, report on, and discipline servers should not be equated with an expansion of consumer power as such. On the contrary, customers' increased leverage over servers through Yelp is ultimately contingent on the discretion of management, whose interests can overlap with but are in other cases antagonistic to those of customers. Simultaneously, while Yelp reviews have generated enormous wealth for the website, it is notable that those who are doing the actual work of researching, writing, editing, and uploading the reviews have not profited from this wealth.

Why then do so many people spend so much time performing work that others profit from but for which they are not remunerated? What do reviewers expect to achieve with their reviews, and, more importantly, are these expectations met? Whereas, as we will see, users enjoy writing reviews, this chapter focuses on the limitations of consumer power through examining the circumstances in which managers respond to, and ignore, Yelp reviews. I argue below that consumer power is vastly overstated and that the customer is most certainly not "always right."

YELP REVIEWERS

This study is informed by dozens of conversations that I have had with Yelp reviewers, restaurant servers, bartenders, managers, and owners, as well as my own experiences working in three restaurants in the 1990s, well before the arrival of Yelp. Additionally, from the winter of 2014 through the spring of 2015 I surveyed 31 Yelp reviewers online. Because a substantial portion of Yelp's business reviews are written by repeat reviewers, I sent 64 of my 101 survey queries to so-called "Elite Reviewers." As Michael Luca (2011) has shown, readers are more likely to read and take seriously reviews written by "Elites," reviewers who are deemed reliable, detailed, and prolific. Yelp, recognizing that the site's traffic corresponds to the perceived reliability and detail of the reviews, encourages such reviews by conferring "Elite status" on their writers. "Elite status," which can be withdrawn from users if their rate of reviews declines, not only accords users the esteem of formally recognized expertise but also rewards them with a variety of exclusive event invitations often featuring free food and drinks. Notably, I experienced an exceptionally high response rate from Elites, whom I messaged from my personal Yelp account.[3] Of the 64 I queried, 23 people, or 35.9 percent, responded, sometimes in substantial length and detail. By contrast, only 8 non-Elites, or 21.6 percent, responded of the 37 I messaged, and non-Elite responses were typically far shorter than Elite responses. I also received several responses informing me that the user is uninterested in participating in the research or unable to because he or she is a Yelp employee. In general, the more reviews users had written the likelier it was that they responded to my survey requests. While this positive correlation might be attributable to the amount of time a user spends on Yelp or how much the user enjoys writing, I attribute the exceptionally high rate of (frequently highly detailed) responses from Elite reviewers at least in part to these reviewers' repeated identification with and sense of responsibility for what several respondents described as "the Yelp community."

It is also important to again note that this study does not aim to present a statistically representative quantitative account. Due to the enormous, and perpetually shifting, diversity of data involved, conducting such a study would be exceedingly onerous. More importantly, I am not seeking to present such an invariably broad statistical study but am instead aiming to explore several relevant themes and illustrative aspects of this story in relative depth in order to gain insight into not merely shifting business trends but the present nature of contemporary capitalism, at least in one regard, itself.

Based on my research, Yelp users are inspired overwhelmingly by the desire to help others, specifically defined as other restaurant goers. Respondents used the word "help" 31 times, "share" 13 times, "contribute" four times, and "give back" once.[4] Respondents also used the terms "karma" and "altruism" in explaining their motivation to write for Yelp. Bruce articulated this prevailing sentiment of social obligation, writing, "I want to give back to the Yelp community for what they have given me."[5] Notably, respondents have different, though not necessarily mutually exclusive, understandings of just whom they are helping. While some are interested in helping "family and friends," others, like Bruce, are committed to helping the "Yelp community." Or, as Lisa puts it, "I'm on yelp to help other foodies because I use yelp everywhere I go and I tend to only look at Elite reviews as opposed to the ones with less than 50 reviews and have nothing good (or only good) to say." Numerous users are eager to alert readers to problems that they have experienced, affirming their belief that their reviews can hold disappointing restaurants "accountable." Indeed, several respondents stressed their willingness to "call out" poor restaurants or servers. Simultaneously, numerous respondents described their desire to "promote" or "help" restaurants, often local and family-run, that they enjoy.

This general sense of "contributing" or "helping" among Yelp users is consistently accompanied by an often emphatically expressed commitment to professionalism and honorably fulfilling the Yelp "code." Responding to my question regarding possible quid pro quos between restaurants and reviewers,

Robert, for instance, writes, "Some managers have asked me to come back and re-review them on a comp. But I always respond that if I do come back, I have to pick up the check. Even accepting a drink would be a gross violation of Yelp rules and totally unethical." While Robert accurately refers to the explicit rules posted on the website, other respondents invoke an informal and seemingly internalized system of ethics. For instance, Jennifer writes, "I do not like those places and will sometimes call out a business that has attempted to do that (bribe a reviewer with perks). Hooters was doing that for a while, at least the one by my house. I don't like that. I don't give a five-star review for a 15% discount." Sam similarly notes that, "Yes, a server has offered me a free meal for a good review. I declined, because I think that's unprofessional."

Referring to her privileged status as an Elite reviewer with something to lose, Lisa invokes both Yelp's "unwritten rules" as well as the "politics" of the Yelp community, writing, "Sometimes the owners would message me to try their place on the house—I never take those offers because I feel like they are bribes. (Again, you are talking to an avid veteran yelp Elite, not a newbie, we know the 'unwritten rules' and it's all politics in the Yelp community.)" Explicitly referring to Yelp's honor "code," Misha writes:

> I do occasionally have business owners message me after a bad review saying to come back with the next one on the house. I will usually go back but I won't tell them it's me and try to claim the free food. I think it would obligate me to write a good review, and . . . it's not like anyone cares, but a man's gotta have a code.

Notably, this commitment to an individual reviewer code extends to concern about the good reputation of the Yelp community and by extension Yelp itself. Mike asserts:

> Threatening a server with writing a negative review is a major lame move that again, some Yelpers do, which unfortunately gives the rest of us a bad name . . . there are several people that feel like they have some power through Yelp and abuse small businesses and restaurants by writing unfairly critical and/or negative reviews. This is what contributes mostly to the bad rap that Yelp gets, and it's unfortunate that some misguided users and poorly written reviews by some have brought on this stigma.

Similarly, Misha writes, "I have never threatened a server or any other place of business with a negative review. I read of this happening all the time and it (is) quite annoying. It takes away the credibility of the people who are really just taking their time to share their experiences." In fact, using the threat of a bad review appears to be considered more egregious than writing a good review for a perk. Numerous respondents are adamant in their refusal to wield the threat of negative reviews to receive good service or perks. Jennifer writes, "I have NEVER threatened someone with a negative review," and Hank asserts, "I've never used a review as a stick or carrot; that would go against the spirit of writing an honest review."

It should be noted, however, that reviewers' professed desire to help other consumers is facilitated by the ease with which Yelp is used and the rewards it provides. By contrast, the index cards and golf pencils with which diners could anonymously express their feedback were dramatically less popular, and were apparently ignored in the Los Angeles restaurant where I worked. That is, it is difficult to separate reviewers' desire to help others from the illuminated publicity announcing the fact that they are doing so.

Indeed, reviewers are motivated not only by notions of altruism and professionalism but also by prosaic and self-interested rewards. Numerous respondents reported that they enjoy writing reviews for their own sake or as a "fun" "hobby" or "diary," and some of these same respondents also expressed their interest in using their Yelp writings to eventually launch travel blogs. Additionally, several respondents referred to the benefits of having "Elite status." Lisa writes,

> From there on I strived to be an Elite to attend those events and be in that foodie community. The events are social events and you meet cool people that share your love of food or being a foodie and trying the hottest newest restaurants in town. I've been doing it for 6 years and absolutely love it.

And after noting that it is "against the rules" to write positive reviews in exchange for perks, Kenny explains, "What some businesses do is offer something for when you check in with the mobile app as a sign of good will. I've gotten so many random things, from a free appetizer to an actual bottle of wine (that restaurant is no longer in business . . .)."

Reviewers also report that they are motivated by Yelp's system of user compliments and the "useful," "funny," or "cool" votes that can be awarded to reviews. But one of the most significant rewards motivating respondents appears to be the satisfaction derived from being, in effect, an influential food critic. Vonn writes, "I've been offered free meals but I use Yelp as a personal (and public) 'travel' journal. I never mention I'm Yelp Elite or that I've tried X places. I want to experience a restaurant or service just like any other individual and report about it. It's more exciting that way!" Vonn's desire to experience a restaurant "just like any other individual" suggests that she, thanks to the power of Yelp, does not consider herself to be "just like any other individual," but on the contrary enjoys the distinctive sense of power that accompanies being an influential food critic, "playing the expert" incognito. Jennifer also experiences a sense of power from being a Yelp reviewer, but her experiences with this power are more direct and confrontational:

> If you sit down and the server sees you checking into Yelp, that might make them go a little further to take care of you knowing, it is likely you'll be writing a review. But, again, some places don't care about Yelp. Personally, I think it's always a good idea to let the business see you checking in. Maybe they will try a little harder and when you're spending money in a business, you want to be taken care of. At least, I do.

In a similar manner, Vincent refers to the special status—"fame"—that accompanies Yelp reviewers, although he nonetheless disavows this as a personal motive and instead refers to the gratitude that he receives from being a "good person." "I've had workers thank me after I wrote the review. I don't do it for the fame. I do it to let people know there are good people in our world."

There is an apparent contradiction in Vincent's distinction between fame and being a "good person" that is relevant to Yelp reviewers' discussions of their motivations. Namely, Vincent is only able to be a "good person" (i.e., reward employees with kind words in a public forum) because he has the "fame," or power, to do so. If he restricted his gratitude to privately thanking the employee or giving the employee a generous tip, the employee might feel appreciated but would not arguably benefit from having his or her merits openly praised. Similarly, other Yelp reviewers who seek to "help" their favorite local or family-run restaurant or, more commonly, the Yelp community, do so because they perceive that Yelp has granted them the power to do so.

That is, whether reviewers use their power "responsibly"—as almost all of my respondents indicated that they are committed to doing—or "irresponsibly," many reviewers suggest that Yelp provides them with power. In this regard, it would seem that, at least for some, Yelp reviewing can help compensate for feelings of powerlessness; to achieve power necessitates that some had been hitherto lacking, although, to be fair, there are some who have enormous power who seek even more. Yet when considering the relative lack of power most of us experience as workers and—notwithstanding notions of the sovereign consumer—consumers, it is unsurprising that some people would have a desire to assume a "secret identity" with which one can *pretend* to be "just like any other individual." Such a desire for concealed but prodigious power is reflected in the culture at large, for instance through the enormous popularity of films concerning superheroes and other individuals, such as martial artists, who in spite of prosaic appearances and all of the slights and disappointments that we all must regularly encounter are in fact forces to be reckoned with. In fact, it is precisely children—the least powerful of us all—who are likeliest to engage in such fantasies.

While reviewers clearly derive psychological satisfaction from writing reviews, and can, as Michael Luca (2011) has shown, affect restaurant patronage among smaller restaurants, what do Yelp reviews suggest about consumer power in general? Specifically, what effects do reviews have not on fellow reviewers but on the restaurants that are in fact the subjects of these reviews? First, because negative Yelp reviews do harm small restaurants' bottom-line, enough negative reviews could conceivably help drive a restaurant out of business.[6] This would seem to suggest significant consumer power. Yet, it is also true that businesses, even popular ones, go out of business on a regular basis for all manner of reasons. Competition means that you cannot have winners without losers, and whether restaurants fail due to increased rent, increased food costs, increases in the minimum wage, economic downturns, or negative Yelp reviews, restaurants are perpetually going out of business. While the apparent role of Yelp in punishing those restaurants with poor products or service does suggest a form of consumer power, it is just as important to note that quality and service are relative concepts. That is, even if all the "bad" restaurants fail, the very existence of notions of quality and service within the context of a competitive rating system and market society means that new "bad" restaurants will invariably emerge. While such a process can be viewed as a cumulative "race to the top" producing perpetually improving customer service (that is, for those who can afford the frequently higher prices following such improvements), it is important to examine not only the "bottom" left behind in such a race but also the exertion and anxiety of those who are forced to do the running.

There is in fact evidence that Yelp is not a purely neutral arbiter of quality and value but instead discriminates among restaurants on the basis of race. A recent study at the City University of New York compared Yelp reviewers' descriptions of two gentrifying Brooklyn neighborhoods and found that predominantly Polish (white) Greenpoint tends to be described as "cozy" and "authentic" while predominantly African American Bedford-Stuyvesant tends to be criticized for its "atmosphere of dirt and danger" (Zukin, Lindeman, and Hurson 2015). That is, without any necessarily racist intent, Yelp reviewers engage in "discursive redlining," encouraging investment in white neighborhoods at the expense of African American ones (Zukin, Lindeman, and Hurson 2015). Simultaneously, and notwithstanding the fact that Yelp's guidelines advise that "there is no need for threats, harassment, lewdness, hate speech, and other displays of bigotry" (Yelp 2017), racist and sexist posts do sometimes appear on the site and are in some cases not removed by Yelp for up to a week (Rajaee 2017).

How then do reviewers think about the relationship between their reviews and restaurant managers? Jennifer and Mike's responses, respectively, are representative: "I think it varies. Of course they love the good ones. Many will get seriously nasty about the bad ones." And "Some bigger businesses completely ignore Yelp and don't care at all, while I have seen some managers take the time to write back personal notes to each reviewer either thanking them or inquiring on how they could improve." Presuming a wide range of managerial responses, Sam similarly notes: "Sometimes I think managers and workers make fun of the reviews, and other times they take them seriously." And Pia writes, "I know some businesses really do not care and there are some who take it very seriously."

A small portion of respondents, however, suggests that they believe that most managers give serious attention to reviews as a general rule. Lee, for instance, writes, "I am sure most of the managers take note of them," and Kenny writes, "I think most managers live in fear of bad Yelp reviews." And presumably assuming that "managers" are stand-ins for "owners" and suggesting a more intimate relationship between restaurants and reviewers, Vonn writes, "I would think (bad reviews) would feel personal because it's your business and you put your heart and soul into it."

Significantly, while respondents anticipated variation in managers' responses to reviews, almost every respondent asserted that Yelp has helped improve customer service. For instance, Jeff writes:

> Most def. Restaurants are being held more accountable for their food and service. Word of mouth are traveling further due to social media like yelp. This can only help everyone. We want better service and food, yelp can help us do that. (If) businesses want more customers then they can follow recommendations from yelpers. We end up helping each other both ways.

Similarly, Kenny writes, "I think it's created a whole customer-first approach. A decade and a half ago, if a restaurant was in a good location but had bad food/service, they could stick around just from foot traffic of people who didn't have any way of knowing better (short of Zagat guides)."

This apparent contradiction in the belief that management's interest in Yelp varies and the nearly uniform assertion that Yelp has improved customer service is reconcilable when noting that managers consistently pay attention to comments that address service even if they are unconcerned about other forms of feedback. And nearly all respondents answered that they indeed criticize servers when they feel it is warranted. Buster, for instance, writes, "A bartender was terrible, rude to me and my friend. Not friendly, seemed miserable. It made the start of our evening such a downer, I thought to myself this guy needs to get a new job not ruin my night if he's working in the hospitality industry and can't even smile." Taking a broader view, Lisa describes her evolution as a reviewer of servers:

> When I first started yelping I have criticized servers by name because they weren't doing their job. Your job title is a server and you have job duties relating to serving and customer service. I had some servers who have no

> customer service (do not know how to deal with customers), can't serve, or doesn't know how to talk to customer. If you can't be in the business of serving you should find a new job that complements you. But now that I've been yelping for so long, I tend to not criticize a server by name or as much as my first few years because once you reach this level of Elite, you set an example for people and other elites, you tend to be more professional about what you say and you definitely have to watch what you write just because you are well known in the Elite community and you may get criticized yourself or even your Elite status revoked if you are deemed to be abusive. The Elite community is very strong and it's a bond that we all share.

Buster and Lisa's belief that workers who "can't even smile" or "can't serve" customers should "find a new job that complements" them is a commonplace on Yelp. Notably, Lisa's description of her growing sophistication as a Yelp reviewer did not include her questioning her original premise that incompetent (or, what she doesn't seem to consider, possibly recalcitrant) workers find more suitable work. Instead, Lisa has become concerned with setting a good example in order to maintain her reputation as an Elite, which requires that she not be deemed "abusive." Similarly electing to provide career advice to those he criticizes, Hank writes, "Yes, I have criticized servers. There's a certain level of competency I expect out of servers having been one myself. I know the lousy pay and the tiring work, but you don't have a good time being grumpy and then expecting a big tip." Focusing on the importance of server competence, Kenny writes, "I have (criticized servers). Usually for not being responsive or available. I once went to a bar known for its beers and the waitress couldn't answer our questions about specific beers and clearly started making things up." And placing the focus on themselves rather than the workers, Jeff writes, "Bad service ruins a meal for me," while Vonn comments, "The only time I ever felt like I criticized an employee is when I feel they have made repeated attempts to make me feel miserable about a mistake I may or may not have caused. I don't think any good comes out of making your customers feel terrible about what they may or may not have done."

Some respondents appear to take great care to avoid being unfair to servers, though they still apply the core criterion of competence. For instance, Shelley writes that she criticizes servers, "but only when it is abundantly clear that a restaurant is not short-staffed and the server is notably inattentive, rude, or simply incompetent." And Sumer says that she wrote a review complaining about a bartender who twice violated the health code by licking his fingers after squeezing a lemon when preparing a drink. Sumer is herself a server and expressed sympathy with the vulnerability of service workers, but her commitment to, as she saw it, the public health trumped any solidarity she might feel with fellow workers.

The most common justification for criticizing servers is that respondents are aiming to let future diners know "what to expect." While letting other diners know "what to expect" constitutes a key component of the reviewer's perceived duties, this conception of service notably reifies what is in fact a fluid social-economic relationship that is continually being reproduced. For instance, no reviewer suggested that customers' traditional means of leverage, the size of the tip, can function, through rewarding or punishing, to improve future service. Indeed, Vonn's complaints about servers who "make (her) feel miserable about a mistake (she) may or may not have caused" identifies an inherently antagonistic worker-customer relationship yet merely defensively reacts to, rather than interrogates and attempts to overcome, this antagonism. Only one respondent asserted that she does not criticize servers at all. Writing that many customers are "brats and rude," Xin writes that she has only criticized owners, as ". . . the servers are just trying to make some money. . . ."

It is notable that a high majority of respondents have not heard of any cases of servers being punished for negative reviews, indicating that, insofar as they simultaneously perceive that service has improved due to Yelp, most respondents have not encountered, or possibly fully considered, some of the mechanisms used to improve this service. In fact, most respondents suggest that workers do not care about negative Yelp reviews. Mike notes, "I don't think workers particularly care, unless they have a vested interest in the success of the actual business," although some respondents add the qualification that workers might care if they are personally criticized in a review. One respondent notes that she has heard of servers being punished for negative reviews but adds that this was not in regards to anything that she had written. And Pia writes, "I wouldn't say punished, but I would say that I know businesses who have taken things stated in a negative review and approached those individuals directly to rectify the issues," suggesting a fine distinction between rectifying issues (invariably backed by the force of potential punishment) and punishment itself. Similarly, Buster writes, "I am not sure if they were punished. But in the case with the bartender the owner did write me a private message and say thank you for the honest review and what did the bartender look like because he wanted to have a talk with him." Like Pia, Buster divorces having "a talk" with an employee following a customer complaint—discipline backed by the threat of punishment—from punishment itself.

Although respondents nearly uniformly believe that Yelp has helped improve customer service, there appears to be a disconnect between respondents' relatively limited expectations for their service complaints and the actual ramifications of these complaints. This disconnect between limited expectations and significant outcomes can perhaps most clearly be seen in Xin's apparently contradictory statement: "I don't think yelp reviews can actually get someone fired. But I'm assuming there are definitely the cases that it has happened." Xin, the only respondent who refuses to criticize servers, has difficulty imagining that "Yelp reviews" can cause servers to be fired. But, in her more abstract next sentence, her general knowledge of work leads her to correctly speculate that such things are bound to happen, even if she has not been exposed to the specific mechanisms through which they occur.

While my respondents' tones of general judiciousness contrast with the unhinged tenor of some Yelp reviews that attack servers, I would suggest that neither group of reviewers generally believes that their complaints about servers will have a significant impact on these servers. In the first case, respondents, generally focused on warning fellow customers under the premise that bad servers will not change (and should therefore change their line of work), do not appear to be generally aware of the direct role that reviews often play in punishing workers within restaurants. This is an understandable if inaccurate assumption insofar as managers less respond to reviewers to redress customer complaints than they appropriate these complaints in order to more effectively manage workers, a point that will be examined below. This does not suggest that workers are being punished and fired against the will of the reviewers who have of course complained about them in the first place. It does indicate, however, that reviewers, to some degree unwittingly, forfeit ownership and control of their reviews once they upload them onto Yelp and management reads them. In the second, rarer, case of malicious reviews, it is difficult not to conclude that such examples of frenzied vitriol are born of, at least in part, a convergence of entitlement and frustrated powerlessness.[7]

MANAGERS

The Yelp reviews that restaurant managers read are in a sense not the same reviews that customers have written. While reviewers are primarily interested in helping other "foodies," managers have often overlapping but ultimately distinct, and sometimes antagonistic, aims. Restaurant trade journals have explicitly addressed the obstacles and opportunities that Yelp has introduced to management. Writing in QSR (Quick Service Restaurants), Nick DiUlio (2010) quotes consultant and management expert Timothy Howes, who says:

> 'If I hear one more restaurant owner say, "We serve quality food," I think I'm going to scream . . . Quality food is not a differentiator. It has to be more than that. What restaurant would ever tell their customers that they serve mediocre food? . . . In many ways, service quality trumps product quality. . . . You can

> have the best food in the world, but if you have poor service, you're doomed' (pars. 2 and 4).

While Howes asserts that it is vital for restaurants to maintain profit amid an ongoing recession, the service industry has always been defined by its distinct reliance on the output of its workers, which is in many regards the product itself. DiUlio (2010) goes on to quote consultant David Scott Peters, who refers to a study that shows that:

> 'Fourteen percent (of restaurant customers) didn't come back because they were dissatisfied with the service, and 68 percent didn't come back because they encountered "an attitude of indifference." . . . That's 82 percent of your customers not coming back because of you and your people. Your product isn't just your food. It's your people' (par. 7).

The advent of online sites including Yelp, DiUlio continues, has only made it more "critical for owners and operators to tightly monitor the product-quality equation" (par. 16). As Howes explains:

> 'In the old days, dissatisfied customers would tell 10 of their friends that they had an issue with a restaurant. Now, they can tell thousands of people in a matter of minutes. . . . And people will be brutally honest. If you deliver on the brand promise, you'll gain sales. If you stink, everyone will know' (par. 17).

The significance of the fact that restaurants have such a profound reliance on service quality is compounded by the fact that, from a practical standpoint, service is the variable that management can most easily manipulate. That is, most business costs, including rent, food prices, and energy, are fixed. By contrast, managers can in fact increase server productivity, and they do so through Yelp. Notably, however, management uses Yelp in order to advance its own aims, which, again, are not one and the same as, and in fact sometimes conflict with, the aims of customers. For instance, productivity in the service industry includes competence and friendliness but also speed in turning over tables; predictably, the complaint of being "chased" from restaurants, which frequently appears on Yelp, is ignored by management. To be sure, most managers dislike receiving negative Yelp reviews and take them seriously. Holly Machanic (2015), writing in *Restaurant Hospitality*, advises managers to implement the following "game plan" in the event that they receive a bad Yelp review:

- "Call a full staff meeting.
- Come prepared with a few negative (and positive) Yelp posts that are credible and can offer teachable moments to your staff.

- Constructively review the feedback as a group and talk about strategies for improvement.
- Solicit comments from both the front and back of the house to get the whole story.
- Reinforce the mantra that either 'we all succeed together, or we all fail together.' Invested employees are more likely to be committed to the success of the business.
- Make sure everyone on staff understands the protocol for handling a customer service issue and has the autonomy to correct a problem in the moment.
- Be sure to address positive reviews, too. It's important to keep morale up by talking about what's being done well and giving praise.
- Claim your restaurant's Yelp listing so that you can manage your profile and make posts on behalf of your business.
- Implement a policy of responding to both negative and positive reviews. Keep replies sincere and gracious: 'Your feedback is important to us. We hope you'll consider giving us another try.'
- Depending on the nature and legitimacy of the review, you could invite the guest to continue the conversation offline, and discuss options for correcting the situation."

"While unfortunately none of these steps can undo a negative customer experience, they can reduce the likelihood of a repeat occurrence. More importantly, your comments will demonstrate to potential guests who are reading reviews that you're on top of your game."

What goes unsaid in Machanic's "game plan," and is thereby all the more striking, is that she presupposes that the negative Yelp review requiring management to "get the whole story" from staff is a service complaint. While most Yelp reviews address service, they of course also address other aspects of the diner's experience, including prices, ambience, and menu options. Machanic offers no suggestions for responding to criticisms of these factors, as it goes without saying that the very nature of these considerations—notwithstanding the vehemence of customers' opinions—belongs to the exclusive domain of management, who alone determines their legitimacy.

Between the winter of 2014 and the spring of 2018 I interviewed thirty-three restaurant managers, assistant managers, and owners about their attitudes about Yelp.[8] Twenty-four of these interviews were conducted face to face and nine were conducted online, via email or messaging, after I solicited interviews through Facebook. All but two of the in-person interviews were conducted in New York City, New York (the others were conducted in Encino, California), and my online interviews were primarily with managers or owners who work or worked in the Northeast. It is important to note that I need to be cognizant of my own role in these discussions. Managers and owners are in some respects the faces of their establishments, and they are likely interested in appearing reasonable and fair. Managers—or any person in general—are not likely to be entirely open in their dealings with strangers, specifically one who is inquiring about their managerial and operational strategies. Indeed, spokespeople for larger chains—including McDonalds and Starbucks—informed me that all company information not provided on their websites is privileged, while some managers at smaller restaurants appeared quite guarded and reluctant to say anything at all to me. Additionally, I was not seeking to interview managers as a generic stranger or customer. I was instead a PhD candidate—that is, a putative expert in training—with all the social clout that such a position entails. Managers might have attempted to tailor their responses in a manner that not only made them sound admirable but also sought to influence my perception of them and my scholarly investigation of the subject in general. Lest I get carried away with my own "expertise," I need to be attentive to the fact that I was interviewing experts in customer service who are trained in wielding charm and information to advance their aims.[9]

While nearly every interviewee expressed strong opinions about Yelp, their relationships with Yelp are significantly influenced by their specific business models. For instance, on-site owners at smaller restaurants expressed greater contempt for and suspicion of Yelp, and they were more insistent on their right and ability to run their restaurants free of comparatively uninformed customer interference. Off-site owners, including chains, were more likely to utilize Yelp as an ersatz, although not wholly reliable, "mystery shopper." Significantly, the larger the establishment, the more uncritical owners and managers tend to be about Yelp.

Owner Greg's comments are representative of many small restaurant owners and managers' general disdain toward Yelp:

> Don't want to be negative or arrogant, but I've put in over 40 years becoming a restaurant professional and mastering craft. Those . . . who know me can say how well I've done in that pursuit. I have yet to see a Yelper put in the same time and effort to learn about food and drink. There is generally no distinction between personal taste and professional taste—a huge and necessary one in the age of the professional reviewer. Yelp and Yelpers have done more damage to the profession than Food TV, even without all the other crap Yelp has been accused of. I sincerely wish it would either get some real integrity or just go away.

Most managers, however, express a more ambivalent attitude toward Yelp, disliking it but nonetheless acknowledging ways in which they benefit from it. For instance, Diane notes, "I am very much anti-Yelp. But I do use it as a training tool IF the reviews are actually spot-on. I can't think of a scenario in which I would fire someone for a poor on-line review."

Paulo, the owner of a small Italian restaurant, said that he is "not a big fan of Yelp." He ignores complaints about food, saying that Yelp is a powerful tool but reviewers do not have "a lot of judgment." Paulo was particularly frustrated that a reviewer complained about a bad smell in the restaurant although this reviewer ordered his food to go. Interestingly, although Paulo does not reward servers for good reviews or punish them for bad reviews and asserts that there are "no benefits to Yelp," he has confronted his employees about bad reviews. Reflecting this utility of Yelp, Liz, who manages approximately one hundred employees at an international airport, similarly notes:

> I've used Yelp reviews to reprimand employees ONLY when they narrate what has been previously documented. Example: I had an employee with a history of a bad attitude. We coached and counseled her for months and documented her behavior. There were a string of reviews on yelp naming her personally, stating what we had been trying to motivate her to change and we disciplined her accordingly. I also inform my staff of good reviews. Probably more than I inform them of bad.

Elena, an owner of a bistro on Manhattan's Upper West Side, is also generally hostile toward and defensive about Yelp. Although she noted that she looks at Yelp every day, she forcefully asserted, "Yelp is not reliable," and as with several other managers noted that she strongly prefers the (non-anonymous) Open Table site. She went on to say that other restaurant owners in the community "share the same opinions: no one values Yelp reviews . . . anyone could write vicious, malicious Yelp reviews." Arguing that Yelp was designed to engender owner-customer communication, Elena suggested that it instead encourages "personal" and "trivial" attacks, referring to one review that complained that a server placed a glass of water on the wrong place on the table and another review that complained that the server looked at the customer "'in a mean way.'" She noted that she has flagged three reviews, one of which was removed.

Interestingly, considering Elena's daily reading of Yelp, she went on to claim, "In this neighborhood, no one reads Yelp because it's a very old neighborhood" that relies on "word of mouth." Noting that most reviewers either complain of rude servers or of being "chased" from their tables, she emphasizes that her establishment has carefully trained its servers, they "would never" be rude, and that her neighborhood regulars "love the girls" who serve them. Simultaneously, she noted that her restaurant is a "bistro" which derives from the word "fast," and that those who complain about being chased from their tables have unrealistic expectations about how long they should dine.

Notwithstanding Elena's energetic defense of her staff—specifically their training—she conceded that she does check up on complaints about her employees, although she simultaneously asserted that because she is always in the restaurant there is nothing that happens without her knowledge. Throughout the interview Elena stressed the distinction between her neighborhood regular customers and Yelp reviewers, suggesting that the latter exist outside of the "community-driven relationships" that define her business model. Relatedly, Elena complained that venal Yelp representatives, who claim that they "can guarantee (her restaurant) five-stars," solicit her to advertise on Yelp (a complaint made by other owners and managers). That is, although Elena was significantly concerned about what appeared on Yelp, she insisted that she controlled her establishment and characterized both Yelp and its reviewers as an illegitimate force residing outside of her restaurant "community." Confirming EE Vonn's belief that restaurant owners would be personally offended by negative Yelp reviews, Elena also said, "It hurts when someone puts untrue, hurtful reviews, but at least the owners know the truth."

Elena attributed her relative insulation from Yelp—that is, her self-described ability to ignore reviews—to the fact that her restaurant did not have outside investors, and that there was therefore no one (possibly unsympathetic outsiders solely concerned with the bottom line) she needed to please. In restaurants funded by absent investors, she asserted, there is far more pressure on "sheer numbers" and, therefore, more attention is paid to bad reviews.

Elena's suggestion is supported by Anthony, a manager who writes:

> I had an off premise owner for years. Was doing 280–300+ covers a night plus a large party every weekend. I also ran their major tourist attraction restaurant banquet and bar on premise. All while he and his family were on his boat at a well known New England island all summer. His source of information on the operation was checking yelp, trip advisor, and open table reviews. I lost a lot of good staff and was reprimanded as well as threatened to lose my job because 1 out of say 500 diners posted they had a sub par experience. This would then lead to a week long witch hunt and staff investigations to find the server who had that one table.

And John, who manages a medium-sized Upper West Side restaurant, says that Yelp has been useful in "enforcing protocol." For instance, after reading a Yelp review that complained about the reticence of his bar staff, John required his bartenders to proactively greet customers. By contrast, Yelp reviews that complain about food are sent to the general manager, and it is unclear what, if anything, is done with them. Like Elena, John has a generally hostile and untrusting attitude toward Yelp and its users. For instance, he described a customer who had complained about being charged for toast and, even though the charge was removed, upon leaving yelled: "'I'm going to write a bad Yelp review!'" John also said that some restaurants pay for positive reviews and that some of his competitors have written negative reviews about his restaurant and that Yelp refuses to remove these reviews. As in other cases, John's skepticism about the reliability of Yelp does not prevent him from employing it to help manage his staff.

There are, however, limits to some managers' willingness to use Yelp to improve service. A manager of a large delicatessen told me that he had been considering introducing a contest in which servers who received a certain number of positive Yelp reviews would receive gift cards, but he abandoned the idea when he realized that it would incentivize servers to make quid pro quos with customers (e.g., providing free drinks or extra dessert in exchange for positive reviews). Indeed, managers frequently describe Yelp as a "tool" in which benefits are determined by how, and for whose interests, reviews are used.

When I introduced myself to restaurant managers and said that I was interested in speaking with them about Yelp, several managers enthusiastically told me that they "hate Yelp" and would be happy to speak with me. Again, even these managers, notwithstanding their contempt for Yelp, admitted that they use negative Yelp reviews to monitor and sometimes punish their employees, with one manager of a restaurant-bar saying, "It's the industry standard." However, only one manager—an assistant manager—told me that a Yelp review led to an employee being fired. The reviewer complained that the restaurant's bartender was using her smartphone instead of tending to the reviewer. After reading the review, the manager checked the establishment's security tape from the bartender's shift, confirmed that the bartender had in fact been on her smartphone, and fired her. The assistant manager additionally told me that his establishment is generally uninterested in Yelp reviews that criticize the food and drinks.

I also queried ten national chains regarding their use of Yelp. Although most of these chains would not reveal this information to me, Faith, a manager at the global chain Le Pain Quotidien, told me that it is that chain's corporate policy to systematically review all Yelp reviews, and that she confronts employees about negative reviews and motivates workers with positive ones. While she did note that none of her employees had been fired due to negative reviews, she asserted that reviews can affect how she awards shifts. Faith seemed proud of the company's policy, not, I speculate, due to its disciplinary utility per se but due to what it seemed to express about the company's interest in satisfying its customers, although these are of course not mutually exclusive goals. Simultaneously, she noted that nonservice related complaints are sent to the home office. The effects of reviews on shifts were also discussed by the manager of Machiavelli's, an Upper West Side restaurant, who emphasized that she rewards rather than punishes employees who receive good reviews by awarding them with more desirable shifts. It is reasonable to add, however, that if an employee is receiving better shifts another employee is necessarily not, illustrating how Yelp reviews can motivate staff to compete with one another and thereby increase their productivity.

A representative of the Global Restaurant Group, who requested to be interviewed anonymously, also noted that her chain "absolutely" relies on Yelp reviews, in addition to Trip Advisor and internal mystery shoppers, in its management of employees. While stressing that management knows that reviews can be unfair and therefore wants "both sides of the story," she said "they will absolutely talk to employees who got criticized, and managers put reviews on bulletin boards to boost morale," and that "Yelp shapes the culture of the company." Cautioning that Yelp reviewers are far less reliable than internal mystery shoppers who are company employees, she explained, "You confirm reviews with security footage and past receipts in order to tell if they're legit. A red flag is if a reviewer asks for a gift card." Nevertheless, the company has benefited from Yelp, as "An email goes out every week (celebrating Yelp) 'all stars.' (And managers) talk about (good reviews) at shift meetings." Yelp has assisted the company in improving worker productivity, she asserts, insofar as it helps "bring issues to light."

SERVERS

In addition to numerous informal conversations with friends, acquaintances, and students who are current or former servers, I conducted interviews with twenty-nine restaurant servers, one cashier, and five bartenders. While only one manager knew of a case in which a Yelp review precipitated a firing, all but six employees I spoke with knew of someone (though not necessarily at his or her restaurant) who had been fired because of a negative Yelp review. Unlike reviewers, then, most of the employees I spoke with are concretely aware that those in their profession could lose their jobs due to Yelp.

I must here again address the possible influence of my own role in this process, as I am distinctly intervening in the lives of those I am engaging rather than merely recording a preexisting social phenomenon from which I am detached. I interviewed seventeen servers, one cashier, and five bartenders in their places of work, frequently in effect as a customer, as it proved too impractical (due to servers' busyness and potential fear of being monitored by management) to interview employees in their workplaces without sitting down and taking the time to catch them in down moments (that is, without becoming a customer).[10] In many of these cases, I had not yet paid for my purchase or left my tip when I questioned the employee, and, moreover, servers and bartenders are trained to accommodate customers, all of which might have consciously or unconsciously encouraged them to provide me with what they surmised I wanted.

Just the same, the descriptions provided in my in-restaurant and in-bar interviews were consistent with the eight interviews I conducted outside of my interviewees' workplaces and the four I conducted online. Excluding online interviews, all but six of my interviews were conducted in New York City, New York, with the remaining six being conducted in Hollywood, California; Cambria, California; and Encino, California. Several employees described regular staff meetings that were oriented around Yelp reviews. In most cases, managers read aloud both positive and negative reviews, and in one restaurant the manager only calls meetings after a negative review has been posted and then directs his staff to immediately write positive Yelp reviews in an effort to crowd out the negative one. By contrast, one server told me that his manager discourages his employees from even reading Yelp in an effort to shield his restaurant from the influence of the website.

Workers have varied, and often mixed, feelings about Yelp. Mike, a waiter in Lower Manhattan, told me that Yelp has helped him. After reading repeated complaints that his restaurant serves pink, and therefore supposedly undercooked, turkey burgers, Mike began preemptively warning customers that the turkey burgers are pink due to the way in which they are seasoned. Sumer, the server I spoke with who also writes Yelp reviews, said, "We don't consider it (Yelp) the problem. A stupid manager or customer is the problem." Continuing, she noted, "If you're generally seen as a reliable server, you would be unlikely to hear about it (a bad review)." Unreliable servers, she continued, will be questioned "more seriously" if they are the subjects of a negative Yelp review: "'Hey, did anything weird happen Friday night?' And more direct managers will just say: 'Hey, what happened?'"

Yet, I have been provided repeated accounts of employees being fired due to negative Yelp reviews. In one example, a waitress who was unpopular with management was fired from a Brooklyn restaurant after her angry ex-boyfriend posted a vicious review of her. Notably, the managers reportedly knew that the review was fabricated but fired her anyway. Another server told me, via Facebook, "I was once yelped about in a terrible and completely untrue way (very disturbing review). Reviewer had no history, no followers, one single review (about me) and their name was quite nearly that of a known enemy. I was suspended for 5 days." And a waitress at Luke's Bar and Grill told me that a coworker had just been reprimanded for a Yelp review that complained that the employee had not been paying attention. In addition to the reprimand, management demanded that the coworker read and "think about" the reportedly "mean" "five-paragraph" Yelp review. This server said that fear of bad reviews and similar punishment has made her more attentive. Notably, I also interviewed this server's manager, who complained about Yelp, noted that he nevertheless uses it as a managerial tool, but omitted the server's story of her colleague's recent reprimand and punishment.

Similarly, Monika, who works at a downtown restaurant, said that Yelp "makes you work harder," as the identities of the workers described in Yelp reviews are self-evident. She, for instance, is "easily identifiable" as the "blonde" hostess. Describing Yelp as an "invisible guiding hand," she notes that employees' awareness of Yelp means that "You were going to perform your best. You don't want something written about you." Other workers noted that the fear of a bad review produces "more pressure to perform" and "makes you more considerate." Max, a longtime server in Los Angeles, told me that customers have requested to be seated in his section because they have seen him praised on Yelp. While appreciating the compliments of customers, Max notes that his online popularity has introduced pressure to live up to expectations. Remarking that other servers resent his popularity, Max also observed that Yelp has changed the restaurant industry through either making servers work harder or making them embittered.

Another server, Alfred, wrote to me:

> We all read the reviews, good and bad, it was quite easy to figure out who was being talked about. Most of my working associates hated Yelp. I know of two servers that lost their positions because of the reviews. Unfortunately the reviews were correct and those that lost their jobs probably deserved some sort of action, perhaps not losing their jobs, but something needed to be done.

This concession to putative fairness was echoed by several other servers, including a server at the Hummus Place chain who noted that it is "usually bad" servers who have gotten into trouble, including suspension, due to bad reviews. As in other cases, management at Hummus Place cross-checks negative reviews, when possible, with their computerized shift records. While this server distinguished herself from her "usually bad" colleagues, she nonetheless asserted, "Yelp is good for the chain but definitely adds stress."

It would be a mistake, however, to conclude that negative Yelp reviews merely serve as pretexts for what management wants to do anyway. After all, workers are employed at will and can be fired at any time. The relevance of management's use of Yelp in firing employees less concerns these terminated employees than the remaining employees who have been made acutely aware of a new and concrete *fireable* offense made possible by a ubiquitous and sometimes arbitrary customer surveillance system. After all, employers do not wish to and cannot fire all of their employees. What they do want is to make their employees more productive, and Yelp, making employees more anxious and vulnerable, achieves this end.[11]

Here we can see a particularly significant difference between Yelp reviews and in-house mystery shoppers. The latter would visit and report on restaurants irregularly in order to maintain an element of surprise. Drawing on my own experience, workers would often relax following a visit and report, as it was assumed, correctly or not, that the corporate office would not repeatedly send a mystery shopper to the same restaurant within the same month, let alone the same week. I recall breathing a sigh of relief with one of my managers following a report, assuming that we apparently would not have to worry about being monitored again for some time. Additionally, workers could, and did, guess which of their customers might be a mystery shopper. Regardless of the reliability of such guessing, there was an assumption that a solitary middle-aged diner ordering an entree very well might be a mystery shopper while a teenager sharing fries with her girlfriends would not. Through Yelp, by contrast, anyone and everyone could be a reviewer. The temporary increase in alertness and anxiety experienced when interacting with suspected mystery shoppers has therefore increasingly become permanent, raising productivity and forcing workers to be "on" for longer periods of time, even when they might need a reprieve from the interpersonal and practical demands of dealing with customers. Insofar as they are forced to project, and often amplify, a happy, charming, and deferential attitude to customers who they generally do not know—and at times resent—we can describe service workers as being alienated from themselves. The duration and intensity of this alienation have been substantially increased through Yelp.

THE CUSTOMER IS ALWAYS RIGHT (AS LONG AS THE MANAGER SAYS SO)

At first glance, the significance of Yelp is that it has empowered customers at the expense of servers. Indeed, when compared to customers' traditional means of leverage over servers it becomes clear that Yelp provides customers with a more intensive and invasive form of control over those who serve them. Reporting directly to Yelp's online audience (and indirectly to managers themselves), online consumer managers diminish workers' power. For instance, conflicts between workers and customers previously generally occurred and concluded in real time, providing servers with some leverage since servers can, for instance, delay, deny, or sabotage service or merely "talk back" to rude customers (Paules 1991). Ironically, even tipping has provided servers with a mechanism for asserting themselves against difficult customers. While tipping, to be sure, reflects and potentially reinforces the customer's putative economic and social superiority over the server (Paules 1991, 44), tipping simultaneously introduces opportunities for servers to challenge and invert this relationship through rejecting tips from hostile or parsimonious customers and in some cases refusing service altogether

(Paules 1991, 37). Rejecting her role as an economically dependent supplicant whose competence is subject to customers' evaluations, one waitress in Greta Paules's *Dishing It Out* told a customer who had threatened to stiff her, "'You need it more than I do, baby'" (Paules 1991, 37). By contrast, in online consumer management customers retroactively and unilaterally attack workers via anonymous reviews aimed not at engaging servers or even improving service per se but at warning other customers to avoid "bad service."[12] Servers cannot chase down and reprimand hostile reviewers in the manner that servers have followed customers into parking lots to reject insultingly small tips and, by extension, negative and offensive evaluations of the servers' competence or attitude. As such, online consumer management has helped alter the terrain of conflict between servers and customers as the mere potential of a Yelp review can discourage servers from defending themselves against difficult customers. Instead of engaging in battles with customers as service is being provided and servers still maintain relative leverage vis-à-vis customers, servers must now increasingly succumb to the judgment of managers who mediate customers' online complaints. In Paules's account, for instance, servers working the graveyard shift could stand up to obnoxious customers in part because there was no manager on duty. However, the presence of Yelp means that customers no longer need a manager on site to discipline workers. Posting a Yelp review is in fact arguably easier than finding out when a manager is in and calling to complain as one would have done before Yelp. And many unsatisfied customers would have been reluctant, whether due to time considerations or social uncomfortableness, to confront a manager who was on site. Even in restaurants that provided "How are we doing?" cards, there was no guarantee from the customer's perspective that such cards were acknowledged, and such complaints were undoubtedly not shared with the public. Rather than being deposited into an on-site container and seen only by management, Yelp reviews are (generally) permanently posted in a public forum of like-minded and supportive readers, an advertisement for or against a particular restaurant and, often, server.

While Yelp has provided customers with increased control over servers, it nevertheless should be stressed that such control is ultimately subordinate to and contingent upon servers' actual bosses: restaurant managers. As we have seen, many employers resent and bridle against Yelp's encroachment into their managerial domains. But regardless of the extent of the Yelp backlash, which in some cases is expressed through Yelp "boycotts," the high majority of restaurants do invoke Yelp reviews to manage their employees. A then paradoxical benefit of referring to Yelp reviews when disciplining employees is that managers can invoke an outside authority along with the mantra "the customer is always right" to both reinforce their discipline and tacitly encourage employees to not resent their bosses since such discipline represents a putatively external mechanism that is out of the bosses' hands.

However, as shown above, managers are in fact highly selective in how they respond to Yelp criticisms, ignoring, if only of necessity given slim profit margins, complaints about prices and focusing nearly exclusively on nonchasing-related comments about service. But even here managers reserve their right to interpret customer feedback as they see fit. For instance, Mike was reprimanded after a Yelp review praised him for his deep knowledge of opera, indicating that the server had engaged in a relatively long conversation with the customer. From the customer's perspective, Mike's erudition and, more importantly, attention were appreciated. Indeed, Yelp reviewer Jennifer echoes numerous other reviewers when writing that servers should "make me feel important and valued." And while not a single Yelp reviewer agrees with the statement, "the customer is always right," the majority of respondents agree with a version that they amended: e.g., "the customer is always right (within reason)." Mike's manager, however, was more interested in not allowing customers to become too comfortable and in clearing tables than in making this customer "feel important and valued."

It is of course debatable whether it is within "reason" to expect Mike to discuss opera with his customer, even if this conversation did not prevent Mike from tending to other customers. What is more relevant, however, is that the same manager who refuses to indulge a customer who wants to converse with his waiter would in all likelihood appear to indulge a customer who complained about a server. Firing an employee who provided poor service (assuming that this is what the customer even wants) is a far greater indulgence of customer rights than permitting a server to chat with a customer during a lull. But of course, irrespective of the assumptions and motives of Yelp reviewers, management appropriates reviews not to fulfill customers' demands but to increase their control over workers, phenomena that are not one and the same and which, on the contrary, are at times mutually exclusive.

NOTES

1. A version of portions of this discussion was published in *New Labor Forum* (2014).
2. And not just restaurants of course. The manager of my former apartment building once contacted me asking if I could write a positive review of her for the management company's Yelp page, noting that she had received some negative reviews and that her bosses "take these things very seriously." Needless to say, her bosses were far less interested in my concerns about the cost of rent.
3. My Yelp account contains five reviews, and it was brought to my attention that at least some of my respondents read these reviews after receiving my message. Unlike most other Yelp accounts, my profile does not contain a personal photo, yet I nonetheless surmised that having an active account, and thus being seen as a member of the "Yelp community," provided me access that "cold messages" from an inactive account would not have.
4. I am excluding uses of these terms in unrelated contexts; e.g., when respondents wrote, "I hope this helps."
5. I have not made revisions to written responses other than correcting spelling for clarity and anonymizing names.

6. The trade journal *Restaurant Hospitality* (2015) notes that "[N]ew research indicates that negative posts can predict an impending restaurant's closure with 70 percent accuracy."

7. For instance, Emily S. concludes her review by addressing the cashier who offended her, "Fat girl with glasses: yes, you damn well do know which muffin is better—chocolate marble or blueberry . . . you know you scarf 'em all down after the place closes . . . you can't hide it!!!" There are entire websites and talk show segments that are devoted to examining for comic effect such infuriated reviews.

8. Although managers and owners are often not one and the same, I am ignoring their differences in favor of focusing on their common and salient attitudes toward Yelp, which are informed by the fact that both groups manage workers. Such attitudes, discussed below, additionally tend to be influenced more by the size of the establishment than by whether the respondent is an owner or a nonowning manager. Although there are indeed managers who are scrutinized by Yelp-consulting owners, I am, further, primarily interested in evaluating Yelp's disciplinary effects on labor, which, unlike management, is not a direct arm of ownership and is directly responsible for producing profit.

9. Several interviewees provided me with complimentary coffee and offered food.

10. Bartenders, by contrast, generally had more space and time to themselves and were freer to talk while at work, even when I came solely to conduct an interview.

11. This concept of fireability is informed by Nicholas De Genova's discussion of a "deportation regime" in which the state's aim is to render undocumented migrant workers a highly vulnerable, and thereby highly exploitable, workforce not through mass deportations but through the perpetual threat of deportation (De Genova 2005).

12. The complaint of "bad service," when it is designed to warn other customers, typically presupposes that service is a static fixture rather than the product of relational and situational interactions. Today's "bad service" could be tomorrow's "good service" if the worker's headache has gone away, the customer is in a less impatient mood, or if the floor is properly staffed.

Chapter Four

Rate My Professors

'A's (and Debt) for Everyone

As with Yelp, the website Rate My Professors (RMP) provides an example of the way in which unpaid Internet users, in this case students, help manage labor in the modern workplace.[1] At first glance it is not necessarily apparent that RMP lends itself to a useful comparison to Yelp. While both websites are based on unpaid user-generated reviews, the subjects and contexts of those reviews are significantly different. Yelp reviews address numerous aspects of a bar or restaurant (among other businesses) and sometimes ignore service altogether. Yelp reviews that do address service discuss workers who are not necessarily highly trained and occupy a relatively low position—in prestige if not necessarily remuneration—in the wage labor hierarchy. By contrast, RMP focuses on college and university instructors per se.[2] While servers evaluated on Yelp are not typically blamed for poor food let alone high prices, instructors on RMP are generally held responsible for nearly all aspects of the student's experience in the course. Further, college and university instructors, who spend years mastering recondite scholarly canons that they then teach to students, are often accorded substantial prestige, which can create more jarring juxtapositions between the sometimes vicious RMP reviews and their subjects and the sometimes vicious Yelp reviews and theirs. We might say that the least eminent adjunct instructor, who if nothing else has the power to assess and grade students, receives more social recognition than the most successful restaurant server. Dining establishments, with their implicit and frequently explicit commitment to customer service, are paradigmatic customer-service industries. By contrast, the university, retaining traces of the feudal era in which it emerged, is to some extent characterized by a commitment to duty and hierarchical relationships shaped by mutual obligation. Even today there are parts of the world where students rise from their desks when their professors enter the room, a gesture of deference that would leave a restaurant server nonplussed.

While this chapter focuses on colleges and universities in the United States, where society is comparatively informal, we should not equate restaurant service relations with college and university service relations. In fact, it is the two industries' qualitative differences that can help make a comparison between them instructive. On one hand, these industries' disparities do not prevent us from identifying a shared phenomenon concerning the ways in which consumer or student expectations discipline labor. On the other hand, their disparities—not only in popular assumptions but also in sociological contexts and settings—allow us to examine the different ways that this same phenomenon manifests. Thus, what does it imply for the worker that, according to my surveys, while only some restaurant servers look at Yelp, most adjunct instructors look at RMP? Further, how are the differences between restaurants and colleges and universities reflected in those institutions' attitudes toward consumer-based websites evaluating their staffs? If restaurant managers' ambivalence toward Yelp suggests a turf war between managers and customers over control of operations, should we expect an even greater turf war between departments and RMP users given the very question of whether students should even be defined as customers?

As with our discussion of Yelp, we need to highlight the ways in which contemporary production and consumption, specifically in the form of online reviewing, mediate one another. Reviewers, or online prosumers, should not be thought of as dupes stricken with a false consciousness that drives them to pursue ostensibly counterproductive interests determined by business owners. Although reviewers undoubtedly react to site designs and directives, reviewers have discretion, even if limited, in the ways that they react to sites. Notwithstanding the dubious symbolism of the chili pepper (abandoned by RMP, as noted, in 2018) as an indicator of instructor "hotness," there is evidence, for instance, suggesting that students' use of it nevertheless reflected a surprising—and unaccounted for, by most RMP critics—level of consideration and even arguable rebelliousness. Responding to my question "What more accurately describes your general experience?" twenty-six students (81.5 percent of respondents) selected the answer, "Instructors who are interesting and engaging tend to seem more physically attractive." Only five (or 18.5 percent) answered, "Instructors who are physically attractive tend to seem more interesting and engaging." Twelve respondents (57 percent) award an instructor with a chili pepper when "The instructor, regardless of my opinion of his or her class, is physically attractive." Four respondents (19 percent) award a chili pepper when they "like the instructor and use the chili pepper to reward the instructor regardless of his or her attractiveness." One respondent (4.76 percent) agreed with the statement, "It's random/a joke. I don't take the chili pepper seriously, and just award it for fun." And four students (19 percent) selected "Other," with one respondent writing, "I don't (award chili peppers), I think it is totally inappropriate," and another writing, "If an instructor is a great professor AND is physically attractive, I'll use the pepper. If he or she is a terrible professor but attractive, I won't use it." That is, under 60 percent of all respondents who have awarded chili peppers do so only when they find the instructor physically attractive. Over 40 percent of respondents either do not use the chili pepper or award it on their own terms, suggesting that reviewers attempt to make sites, and site meanings, their own. Nevertheless, because such mediation occurs within highly disparate relations ultimately based on unequal property ownership, there are structural limits to such efforts. That is, if users at times make sites such as RMP and Yelp their own, these sites—and dominant social relations in general—to a far greater degree make users' contributions *their own*.

DEBATING RMP

RMP was created by John Swapceinski in Menlo Park, California, during the 1999 dot-com boom. It has survived competitors such as PassCollege, ProfessorPerformance, Reviewum, and RatingsOnline, and it is the most popular professor ratings site today, featuring far more reviews and monthly visits than current competitors including MyEdu (formerly Pick-A-Prof), Koofers, Uloop, and RateMyTeachers. The site was sold in 2005 and again in 2007 to mtvU, a division of Viacom. Featuring over 19 million reviews of 1.7 million professors (Rate My Professors 2018), the site allows students to research prospective instructors and rate their own on 1–5 scales measuring "overall quality" and "difficulty," with an accompanying happy face representing "Good Quality" (3.5–5), an emotionless face representing "Average Quality" (2.5–3.4), and a sad face representing "Poor Quality" (0–2.4).[3] Students can also write a 350-character description of the instructor and course.

While the validity of RMP reviews has been subject to much debate, as in the case of Yelp I am much less concerned with RMP's reliability than with its effects on workers, in this case untenured instructors—and specifically adjuncts—at colleges and universities. Yet it will nonetheless be instructive to examine these debates, as their language and assumptions reveal some of the key tensions characterizing higher education in the neoliberal era in general and the role of contemporary university and college instructors in particular.

A central line of debate in the discussions of RMP concerns the site's validity in assessing instructor effectiveness, since, for instance, anyone (including people, such as professional rivals, who have not taken a class with the instructor) can write a review. However, many of the criticisms of the site's ostensible lack of validity are flawed. One common claim is that reviews are shaped by the site's allegedly inherent selection bias, since only students who either love or hate an instructor would presumably go through the trouble of writing (and creating an instructor page where one does not exist) a review. However, student reviewers I surveyed frequently asserted that they write reviews as a service to other students in return for the information that they themselves have received from the site. RMP itself encourages student reviewers to "pay it forward" and possibly "save" a fellow student's semester through having "fun" on the site (RMP 2015), while also noting that 60 percent of all reviews are positive with a score of 3.5 or higher (RMP 2015; Epstein 2006). Some reviews consist solely of descriptions of the assignments students should expect to complete and make little mention of the instructor at all. That is, the same commitment to community and ethos of "helping" others that characterizes many Yelp reviewers characterizes RMP reviewers, suggesting that fears of selection bias are likely overstated. Furthermore, students also write reviews when they believe that a professor has been unfairly rated on the site; that is, students knowingly correct for perceived bias or unfairness (Otto, Sanford, and Ross 2008). Student reviewers additionally talk with other students who have not written reviews and can therefore sometimes be seen as representatives of more general classroom views rather than as emotional statistical anomalies (Otto, Sanford, and Ross 2008).

Perhaps the most serious charge of RMP's lack of validity is contained in a broader criticism of student evaluations in general. "It doesn't much matter what the questions are, says Linda B. Nilson, director of the Office of Teaching Effectiveness and Innovation at Clemson University. . . . 'What they really measure is student satisfaction. . . . They bear no relationship at all to learning'" (Berrett 2015). This apparent conflict between student satisfaction and learning might appear reconcilable (e.g., entertained students might be engaged ones, just as satisfied students might be satisfied that they improved their understanding of the subject) if it were not for long-term studies demonstrating that student satisfaction is in fact based on grades and that the higher the grade and satisfaction with the instructor the more likely it is that students will fare poorly in future courses (Poropat 2014). According to Arthur Poropat (2014, par. 7), "This confirms the fears of educators: students' evaluations are linked with current grades, but also with students' failure to learn things they need for the future. So, a student who is happy with their grade and teacher should worry—they may not have learnt that much." Moreover, Poropat (par. 11) continues, "there is independent evidence that students who think highly of themselves blame the teacher if they get bad grades."

That is, beyond the fact that students are often unequipped to meaningfully assess the instructor—for instance, concerning the instructor's knowledge of the subject (Poropat 2014)—student evaluations are inherently flawed insofar as they seek to measure data that are not only incommensurate but in some regards mutually exclusive. For instance, a rigorous instructor who is a demanding grader might not generate student satisfaction but very well might promote student learning.

The fundamental problems characterizing student evaluations are only intensified on RMP since that site explicitly measures—and thereby encourages students to think in terms of—"difficulty" and, until recently, "hotness." Arguing that high quality ratings on RMP less reflect student learning than perceived instructor easiness and attractiveness, Felton, Koper, Mitchell, and Stinson (2006, 2) note:

> Our statistical analysis of scores and postings from RMP suggests that student evaluation of teaching (SET) is influenced by more than just intrinsic quality of instruction (Felton, et al., 2004). Specifically, Quality scores at RMP show a strong positive correlation with the perceived Easiness of the course and the Hotness of the professor. In other words, a large percentage of American college students who post professor evaluations at RMP consider courses to be of high quality when the professor is attractive and the course is easy.[4]

And Janice Fiamengo (2013, par. 4), referring to the findings of Valen Johnson's *Grade Inflation* (2003), writes:

> [S]tudent responses to their university experience have been corrupted by an entitlement mentality about grades. Because students tend to excuse poor performance by pointing to external factors, they often blame their teachers when marks are lower than expected—when, as one student wrote on the site, they are "completely blindsided by a bad grade." The problem is acute in the grade-inflating Humanities disciplines, where an element of subjectivity is always present and where one instructor's decision to give higher marks than the material deserves—whether from pedagogical principle or to grease the wheels of a happy classroom—creates pressure on other instructors to do the same, and leads to negative evaluations of those who will not. As even a cursory perusal of Rate My Professors uncovers, "Very hard marker" almost always equates to a "Poor Quality" evaluation. This fact alone, as Johnson concludes and as many thoughtful observers can attest, makes teacher evaluations, which are widely used as a ranking method in the modern university, next to meaningless.

Johnson, Fiamengo notes, has argued that the inverse relationship between grades and high ratings has affected different departments unequally, a phenomenon that is encouraging students to abandon the more rigorous natural sciences and mathematics for the arguably more subjectively graded and easier social sciences and humanities.

To be sure, other studies argue the opposite: that easiness ratings are in fact inversely correlated to overall quality, suggesting that RMP reviews do in fact reliably reflect student learning. Notably, however, these studies conclude that RMP evaluations are comparable in this regard to department-issued student evaluations, which of course does not address the critique of student evaluations as intrinsically flawed for measuring in the final analysis student satisfaction. Otto and colleagues (2008, 364) analyzed a random sample of 399 RMP ratings that showed that ratings of clarity and helpfulness are "strongly correlated," and, more importantly, that ratings of easiness are negatively correlated to clarity and helpfulness. The authors conclude that ratings reliably reflect student learning and are not influenced by a so-called halo effect in which, for instance, a student's perception of an instructor's physical attractiveness affects the student's overall assessment of the instructor. In fact, Otto and colleagues argue that their "results have potential implications for instructor evaluation and perhaps promotion, tenure and merit procedures" (364).

Indeed, even Felton et al. (2008) acknowledge that their data showing a positive correlation between quality ratings and hotness and easiness ratings need not indicate causation. The authors allow that one can infer reverse causation, in which students who are inspired by an excellent teacher find the material easy and the teacher attractive. While Felton and colleagues challenge the first claim by indicating that students consistently define "easiness" as constituting a lack of work (8), the authors' suggestion that "most student comments point toward Quality as a function of Hotness and focus on physical characteristics of their professors that could be captured in photographs" (8) is more dubious. In reality, students' focus on "physical characteristics of their professors that could be captured in photographs" does not resolve the issue of the inherent subjectivity of perceptions of physical attractiveness. RMP, until recently, compiled a list of its "10 Hottest" professors every year, and made their photographs public (Lakshmin 2014). Applying the prevailing culturally particular (and frequently arbitrary) definition of conventional physical attractiveness as our point of reference, what is striking about many of these photos is that the teachers resemble neither professional models nor Hollywood actors but instead appear to be utterly "normal" looking, suggesting, again, that some students reward their favorite instructors with chili peppers regardless of the students' aesthetic judgments, that talented and effective instructors do in fact often become "Hot" in the eyes of their students, or that some students might not take the "Hotness" rating as seriously as observers presuppose, findings supported by my survey results.

The Center for College Affordability and Productivity is so sure of the reliability of RMP that it has incorporated RMP reviews into its assessment of top schools in findings published by *Forbes* (*Forbes* 2008). Writing that RMP results are comparable to school-provided student assessments, the study based a quarter of each school's rating on the school's average RMP rating. The study goes so far as to claim that for its purposes RMP is even more valuable than in-school ratings, noting, "the significant advantages of being uniform across different schools, not being subject to easy manipulation by schools, and being publicly available . . . (indicate) that RMP data is a preferred data source for information on student evaluations of teaching—indeed, the largest single uniform data set we know of student perceptions of the quality of their learning experience" (par. 23).

Notably, the Center for College Affordability and Productivity also asserts that "Students are consumers, who, ostensibly at least, attend college to learn and acquire knowledge and skills. The core dimension of the learning experience comes from attending classes taught by instructors. Asking students what they think about their courses is akin to what some agencies like Consumers Report or J.D. Powers and Associates do when they provide information on various goods or services" (par. 16).

This assertion that students are consumers brings us to the crux of the issue. On one hand, the question of whether students are consumers goes beyond the ultimately inconclusive debate over RMP ratings' validity. But, on the other hand, the question of whether students are consumers—and, if they are, what this implies—is in fact subsumed within the debate, indicated, for instance, by the fact that the "RMP is invalid" observers *distinguish* instructor charisma (an attribute associated with student satisfaction) from student learning.[5] It is this question of the relationship between instructor charisma and student learning (i.e., whether they go hand in hand or are unrelated or even mutually exclusive) that provides a keyhole into the assumptions within the debates over RMP and arguably student evaluations in general, as well as, more importantly, the concrete interests underlying those assumptions. That is, those who believe that students are consumers not only adopt a student perspective (that in some cases seeks to not only determine the scope of the learning that is "consumed" but also wishes to be entertained by a charismatic and ideally attractive instructor who will provide the needed grade without much hassle) but by implication also deem instructors mere "service providers" who should in effect keep the customer satisfied. Those who reject the notion that students are consumers, by contrast, struggle to reconcile their dismissal of considerations of instructor charisma with the practical economic realities of modern higher education, in which students are indeed encouraged to "choose" academic paths designed to optimally equip them to compete in the labor market upon graduation—that is, to above all obtain a marketable degree. Specifically, those who cling to a conception of a professoriate that transcends the crude economic calculations of customer service (e.g., those who reject the classification of "service provider" and are willing to fail students when appropriate) still believe that instructors should receive incomes that are nevertheless ultimately contingent upon their universities' economic performance in an increasingly competitive marketplace. This schism between the historic responsibilities of the professoriate and the increasingly countervailing pressures of the neoliberal university has led to contradictory assumptions and expectations among students, department chairs, and instructors, contradictions contained not only in student evaluations in general and RMP ratings in particular but also in the ways these measurements are discussed.

STUDENTS

Unlike Yelp, which allows users to directly message other users, RMP reviews are entirely anonymous and users have no way of contacting other users. In order to access RMP reviewers, I therefore posted requests on approximately three dozen Facebook college and university student group pages, asking students around the country at a variety of colleges and universities to participate in two anonymous surveys accessed through Survey Monkey hyperlinks. Most of these groups were closed, which required that I become a member, and I was necessarily only able to post my survey invitation to groups in which I had been accepted. Nobody, to my knowledge, objected to my posts, in which I identified myself as a City University of New York doctoral candidate conducting dissertation research, even though I typically had little in common with the groups in question, which included several carpooling groups around the country, the Computer Science Club at UC Davis, the University of Denver Queer Straight Alliance, the Center for the Art of Africa and its Diasporas at the University of Texas, Austin, and the New Mexico State University Online Yard Sale Group. On the contrary, several members "liked" my posts, alerted friends to them, and offered me words of encouragement. These student groups had anywhere from thirty to over ten thousand members, and while I cannot determine how many group members saw my invitations, forty-one students completed one general survey and thirty-one completed a shorter survey (focusing specifically on students' use of the RMP "chili pepper"), representing a broad distribution of majors across the humanities, natural sciences, and social sciences and a broad geographic range of U.S. liberal arts colleges and medium- and large-public universities.

Out of forty-one respondents to my general survey, forty have consulted RMP at some point during their college careers, and while several students answered with qualified responses, such as "Yes, though rarely" or "sometimes," thirty-two—or nearly 80 percent—of the respondents answered with no reservations, writing "Yes," "Yes always," "of course," or "definitely." Of these forty-one respondents, thirty-six—or 88 percent—have written at least one review, and several respondents noted that they have written reviews of every course they have taken. There were fourteen respondents who wrote that they were motivated to write reviews by their desire to "help" other students or "give back" to a service that they have benefited from, while a smaller percentage noted that they were interested in helping their instructors or in correcting perceived unfairness in the existing reviews of a particular instructor. To be sure, several respondents indicated that they write reviews because they either loved or hated an instructor: "I only write them for two reasons. I love the professor, or I dread them." Yet, far more respondents wrote that they were motivated by altruism, resembling the stated motivations of many regular Yelp reviewers. Even when students vent about "bad" instructors it is often inseparable from altruistic concerns, as students who do write harsh reviews of their instructors frequently say that they do so not to enact personal revenge but in order to "warn," or provide a "heads up" to, other students so that they can avoid these teachers. Some responses to my question on what leads students to write RMP reviews include: "helping to expand a resource that I use," "To warn other students of bad professor," "trying to warn other students about bad professor," "I reviewed a professor that I thoroughly enjoyed having. I mainly wrote it because I felt the other reviews were too negative for such a great professor—most focused on the difficulty of his class rather than his teaching ability," "(I write reviews for) all of my instructors because good or bad it could help future students when picking out classes like it always does for me," "I want to provide people with the same assistance that I have received," "I write reviews for each instructor. I like to use them so I return the favor for future students," "When a professor is really good or one is really bad. I just want people to know what they are getting into."

For many reviewers, this sense of duty to fellow students is coupled with a conscientious commitment to fairness, resembling the "code" adhered to by many Yelp reviewers. Responding to my question of whether reviewers ever considered in retrospect any of their reviews to be unfair, forty out of forty-one answered "no." Explaining themselves, numerous respondents went into detail describing the unlikeliness of their having written an unfair review in the first place: "No. If it's a bad review I wait a few days before submitting so I can be more objective," "No, all the posts I've written are honest and as objective as possible," "No, I'm always fair with my reviews," "No. I think long and hard before I write them," "No, even if I personally didn't get along with a teacher I tried to keep it fair," "No. Being honest is the only way to go . . . otherwise it would defeat the purpose of rmp." Notably, the one "yes" came with a qualifier reflecting the same conscientiousness characterizing the "no's": "Yes, but not unfair in the traditional sense. I once wrote a review as a favor to a professor, something I later felt was unfair to those reading it. The review described a professor who had the best interests in mind for only a select few."

In fact, respondents were generally taken aback by questions concerning possible RMP impropriety, with all forty-one respondents answering "no" to my question on whether a respondent has ever threatened an instructor with writing a negative review. Several respondents scoffed at the suggestion, writing: "LMAO people do this???? No," "I have not threatened an instructor (with) a bad review. I feel that would make things worse for me, as a student, especially going to such a small school," "I would think they either wouldn't care or would write me up if I suggested such a preposterous thing. If there is a REAL problem, go to the administration, not some dumb website where you can write anything you want without verification," "Absolutely not," "No, never," "That seems absurd; no," "I don't threaten, it's not my style. I'm a man of action and I speak out immediately if I do not agree with someone," "Hah, no." What is striking is that although numerous respondents explicitly use RMP to find easy instructors, respondents bridle at the suggestion that they would use the threat of a negative RMP review to attempt to directly coerce an instructor to provide a good grade. That is, indirect coercion through the marketplace can be consistent with maintaining students' integrity and idealism, while direct, interpersonal coercion is dismissed as either a practical absurdity or an affront to one's dignity.

Respondents were similarly indignant at a question asking whether they have ever offered to write a positive review in exchange for a good grade: "Again, no, and any prof would be idiotic to accept. They could just write themselves a review. Or ten!" "No, because I knew that wouldn't give me a good grade for that," "No, I also feel that if I did offer this, the professor would think less of me, and would not help me out at all," "Lol no," "Wow, I can't believe that someone would suggest that," "That too seems absurd," "No, that's not an option that maintains my integrity."

It is significant that RMP reviewers, unlike Yelp reviewers, do not have screen names or other identifiable site presences and therefore do not collect "friends" or win compliments for being "funny" or "cool." At most, reviewers receive points for being "helpful," although these points accrue to the anonymous review itself rather than the reviewer. That is, RMP reviewers—no matter how many reviews they have written—do not build reputations or receive the various immaterial rewards associated with them. While taking a college course represents a far greater financial and personal commitment than visiting a restaurant, we can nevertheless suggest that the existence of some regular RMP reviewers supports the claim that reviewers on both websites are indeed sincere when they assert that they are motivated to help others, and that some users practice a form of altruism.

HELPING OTHERS DO WHAT?

But what kind of altruism is this? Specifically, what is it that RMP reviewers are helping other users to do? A plurality of respondents (fifteen out of forty) to my question on what characteristics of a review most influence their course selection used terms referring to the ease of the course, including "ease," "toughness," "workload," "hardness," or "grading." Some students were overt in describing their motives: "Honestly, how easy the professor is. Why would I take the same class with a harder professor???" "Hardness of the class. Whether the professor was clear in class or confusing," "If the professor is not difficult or has above a three I will select them," "Average grade," "difficulty of the class, personality of the prof," "easiness and the comments," "easiness." Several other respondents wrote that they look for indications of instructor "fairness," which at least in some cases can be interpreted as a euphemism for ease, as in the comment, "Ease of class and fairness of grading." Another respondent wrote "How fairly the professor grades," bringing to mind the fact that students are not generally privy to everyone's grades in the course—and are therefore unequipped to judge conventional standards of fairness—which again suggests that "fairness" implies "reasonableness" which implies not being too difficult, a demand that numerous students made explicitly. At the same time, other students mentioned the instructor's "helpfulness," "clarity," and "overall quality" (i.e., traditional RMP criteria) as well as approachability and "all of them but the hotness factor." Only one respondent explicitly referred to rigor as a positive trait: "If they mention positive characteristics of a professor. The best kind involve descriptions about a tough but compassionate professor," while another respondent seems to imply a desire for rigor with the vague description: "ability to actually teach." In sum, a substantial portion of students reports that they select instructors based on either ease or traditional RMP categories (helpfulness and clarity) that certainly do not imply rigor, an arguable prerequisite for intellectual development.

As with Yelp reviewers' relationships to other restaurant goers and restaurants, RMP reviewers are more focused on helping other students—which does not necessarily preclude venting about a putatively unfair instructor—than on trying to change instructors' teaching habits. Although sixteen respondents agreed that reviews affected instructors in some manner—some using words like "severely" and "immensely"—seventeen dismissed the very possibility of RMP reviews having an impact on instructors: "None because one bad review out of all their students is not going to change the way they teach. They will still get paid whether they accommodate or not," "None. Most professors don't care about their reviews," "I doubt it does at all." In fact, several respondents questioned whether instructors even looked at their reviews: ". . . I doubt many teachers read them," "Probably not—I doubt they read them." While reviewers were split on whether they believed reviews directly affected instructors, it is notable that of those who believe that reviews do affect instructors, several believe that they do so only indirectly via altering class size: "I think it may affect what classes students choose," and "I think it affects them if the student could choose another class." And in response to another question: ". . . good reviews will draw students to that class, and bad reviews will do the opposite." That is, most students perceive that the source of their power is indirect, a point further suggested by several respondents answering the question of whether instructors read their reviews by simply writing "I hope so" or "hopefully." Regardless of the reality, approximately half of reviewers believe that they are unable to directly change instructors' behavior, but they can, through cooperating with other students via sharing information on RMP, affect instructors' course sizes and thereby potentially affect the instructors themselves.

Interestingly in light of this split, a substantial majority (32–5) of students agreed that RMP has "empowered students." I used the term "empowered" precisely because it is ambiguous, encouraging respondents to interpret the term as they saw fit in order to generate opportunities for them to share their presuppositions regarding their roles as students. Some "yes" responses include: "Yes. They have an outlet if they've been screwed by a professor, and almost everyone has," "Yes. We can control what people think about a professor, and also give the administration a view of what the students think," "Certainly, we have a voice to reach more students than simple conversations through friends on campus," "Yes, we trust each other more than anyone else. You can tell when someone was slacking vs. someone who really thought the professor sucked." Some responses explicitly identify the source of student empowerment as consumer empowerment over teaching: "Absolutely. Classes that were given higher ratings were often full," "Yes it has, it has shifted some power towards the students when wanting to make informed decisions," "Yes. I believe Rate My Professor has empowered students in the sense that (we) now have the ability to walk into a classroom knowing what to expect from a professor. It also allows students to choose professors that work with their particular learning style best," "In a way. I think some students use it to rant or dismiss it as a tool just to get the easiest class, but it certainly has empowered me in getting the most for my money at my university."

Notably, several respondents who agreed that RMP has empowered students were skeptical of the implications of that power: "Yes, to be even more entitled jerks than before," "I think it has opened a forum for students to inform other students, but I think there may be too many angry students who want to voice their anger about a professor or grade they received. In my opinion, we are all adults and sometimes it is our fault we got the grade we did," "Yes but (it) has also contributed to another potential form of online bullying especially to get revenge for poor grades," "Good reviews—that is those reviews of good quality, either positive or negative—have empowered some students. For others, RMP has become an instrument of the dumbing down of academia." Only one respondent, however, responded that RMP does not empower students precisely because it enables them to find easier courses, identifying a mutual exclusivity between students who are defined as learners and students who are defined as consumers: "No. If anything, it may actually set some students back as they seek out easier instructors based off rating."

RMP does not merely encourage students to think of themselves as consumers; it shows that they already do, a fact that is explicable not ultimately to bad or entitled attitudes but to the material economic realities of higher education in which students are making an investment—often a massive one that they will be unable to ever pay back—that they seek to maximize. Paying for registration in itself does not guarantee a passing grade, but professors who are deemed unreasonably demanding will be chastised on the site, a warning frequently heeded by students who want their grades without messy complications.

There is a deep irony in student empowerment on RMP. Student evaluations originated as a consequence of the student protest movements of the 1960s and 1970s. Those students banded with one another to challenge, among other things, the unaccountable authority of instructors who could indeed be unfair, arbitrary, and abusive. However, insofar as these movements failed to upend the hierarchical organization and capitalist aims of even public universities, protests of instructors were ultimately recuperated by administrations that learned to deploy student evaluations as a cudgel to be used against employees.[6] While RMP reflects a very different form and conception of student power from that of the earlier protest movements, we can nevertheless see student cooperation, shared concern, and solidarity within both sets of students. Yet, instead of challenging hierarchies embedded in institutional relationships, as they did during the student movements, students on RMP are primarily working to help one another succeed *within* those relationships.

A decisive difference between today's reviewers and their earlier counterparts is that activity on RMP is divorced from any on-the-ground organization of political power that results from and further engenders relationships, work, and trust. While today's students are undoubtedly politically active on campus, their efforts are frequently either pitted against activities organized by *other* students (dividing students' potential power) or else concern matters of political expression and identity that do not necessarily threaten administrative prerogative.[7] Because RMP in effect *grants* power to students it is, by definition, contingent power reflecting not only the fact that reviewers are materially alienated from a for-profit website that they do not own or have direct control over but also that students are alienated from their own collective political power to address their most immediate economic adversary: the university.

DEPARTMENT CHAIRS

If students are correct that their RMP reviews go generally unheeded by instructors, what do department chairs have to say about reviews? I emailed survey requests to 381 department chairs at 45 schools, comprising 26 public universities, 13 community colleges, and 6 private colleges, including 3 liberal arts schools. I sought to send queries to the same 10 departments at each school, representing a combination of natural sciences, social sciences, and humanities.[8] One hundred two people responded to my requests, completing 24 emailed questionnaires and 78 Survey Monkey surveys. I additionally sent 77 follow-up survey questions to prior survey respondents, to which 44 responded. Over 90 percent of respondents wrote that they consult department-provided student evaluations when hiring, rehiring, or promoting part-time faculty or adjunct instructors. Asked to rate the importance that they place on these student evaluations on a 1–5 scale with one representing "almost no importance" and five representing "great importance," 61 (of 63) respondents replied with an average score of 3.56. Only one respondent selected "almost no importance" while 49 (or 80.5 percent) selected "some importance," "significant importance," or "great importance." Responding to the same question for RMP, only 23 (of 63) respondents replied with an average score of 1.65, with 14 selecting "almost no importance," three selecting "little importance," and six selecting "some importance."

Notably, all six chairs who selected "some importance" work at community colleges, and these respondents displayed a general openness to using RMP, with comments including: "yes," "Some look at it," "I use RMP, yes," and "I do look at students' comments and also show students how to use ratemyprofessor to find good instructors on our campus." Such unapologetic frankness contrasts with the frequently vehement denials of many university and liberal arts college chairs to the question of whether they consult RMP when hiring, rehiring, or promoting instructors.[9] Frequently citing the questionable claim that RMP is used primarily by students who either love or hate their instructors, university and liberal arts college chairs' answers include: "No—absolutely not!" "NO," "NO," "NO!!!" "Absolutely not! Anyone can write on there, and I have, just to test the system," "Never," "Never," "No, no, no!!!" "Heavens no." Some respondents referred to department policies regarding RMP: "No—we actively discourage any engagement with Rate My Professor and there is a general belief that any such informal polling site is inappropriate for a hiring process." Some responses appear defensive: "No. I've never heard of doing this, and in fact most of my colleagues including me have never looked at Rate My Professor, as the end of quarter reviews for each course are hard/good enough." A chair at a liberal arts college wrote: "We do not. I would go so far as to say that about half my departmental colleagues are unaware of the existence of RateMyProfessors." And a chair at a large public university in the Midwest responded, "We do not. I have no plans to consider RatemyProfessors.com in hiring, rehiring or promotion decisions for part time faculty or adjuncts. I have literally never looked at these comments or ratings for any of our lecturers I have hired over the last 5 years as chair."

The adamant, sometimes defensive, tone of these responses further contrasts with numerous responses that concede, sometimes guardedly, that if not chairs themselves then other department members consult RMP when hiring, rehiring, or promoting adjunct instructors: "Not formally. Informally, might look sometimes . . ." "Not officially, however it is not unusual for individual members of a hiring committee to look at this site and report 'red flags' seen in potential hires who have a significant number of reviews posted," "Not as an active policy, yet members of hiring committees often look at this web page," "We don't do so as a department, but I know that some individual faculty members involved in hiring decisions look at this, as one indicator among many," "Only to supplement other evaluation materials; it's not a major decision-making tool." Some chairs refer to only "glancing" at the site: "Not officially but I do glance at them, especially if I sense that there is a problem," "I may glance at it—but I never use it," leaving one to wonder where the distinction lies between "glancing" and "using" and why such insistence (in an anonymous survey) is needed in the first place. Another university chair writes: "Not formally. Some faculty might refer to RateMyProfessors but only out of curiosity as we believe those reviews are problematic," begging the question of what forms the basis of this curiosity over "problematic" reviews, and how faculty distinguish their findings on RMP from their formal decision-making. Other responses include "occasionally," "not officially, no," an elusive "not really," and yet another "Not formally" states: "Not formally. But I've looked there to see whether someone is consistently getting horrible reviews. People generally know who the bad professors are. I also notice when a professor is consistently rated as being 'easy.'"

The ambivalence characterizing many chairs' responses to RMP resembles the ambivalence expressed by numerous restaurant managers' attitudes toward Yelp. In both cases, managers and chairs emphasize the unreliability of unregulated, consumer-based websites, but they nonetheless frequently reluctantly admit (far more so in the case of Yelp) to using the site in order to monitor their employees (and prospective employees in the case of RMP). Department chairs generally note that they consult RMP, if at all, with discretion and primarily rely on it as a "supplement" or, conversely, to identify "red flags" about potentially abusive or unresponsive instructors. I suggest that this ambivalence—vehement criticism in some cases and reluctant acceptance in others—among other things reflects a turf war over control of classroom instruction, including hiring and promotions, between departments and student-consumers. This hypothesis is informed by chairs' frequent insistence on the greater reliability of department evaluations, a point that might be accurate but brings into question why faculty—beyond vague "curiosity"—consult RMP at all. Departments seemingly gain something from looking at the site, but they are often reluctant to admit what it is insofar as doing so would arguably forfeit perceived control of the instructor evaluation process in particular and the workplace in general.

This schism can be seen in the often oblique and occasionally defensive responses chairs provided to the question of whether RMP has "empowered" students. Unlike student respondents, numerous chairs questioned how "empowered" was being defined, and then went on to provide answers: "It depends on what 'empowered' means. I believe that some students enjoy handing out ratings at the end of a class—and they probably experience this process in a way that is similar to liking something on Facebook. However, students don't see any change in instructor's teaching as a result of reviews and sometimes feel like the reviews are hardly read by the institution." Beyond numerous "no's"—including a thunderous "NO!!!"—respondents provided qualified "yes's" that were sure to bring attention back to their own, ostensibly more reliable, reviews: "I think so, but school administered evaluations are more empowering, as they are more official and representative of ordinary students, not just those who like or dislike the teacher enough to comment." This respondent, however, does not show how the official and representative nature of school evaluations are in fact more empowering than RMP ratings. Similarly, one chair is "skeptical of the value of anonymous student reviews. They are rarely specific enough to be of much value," without addressing what type of value is at issue and whom its beneficiaries are. Notwithstanding the fact that some RMP reviews are quite specific, students hardly require specificity to avoid difficult graders. Another chair also seems to either substitute department empowerment for student empowerment or presuppose the student-as-learner perspective, writing that reviews are empowering "Only if they are carried out rigorously and objectively." Again, students looking to avoid hard instructors are not looking for rigor or even objectivity when reading RMP reviews but for clear cues alerting them to whom to avoid.

Other chairs appear to miss the point entirely of many students' conceptions of empowerment, paternalistically writing, "Sites like 'RatemyProfessor' are too unstructured. Students may FEEL empowered, but it is hard to see any effect," "They may make some students feel empowered, but often by giving distorted information," "They probably think they have empowered them, but my personal sense is that the responses are mostly on opposite ends of the spectrum . . . which makes them very stilted." And another chair writes, seemingly self-servingly, "The University's student course evaluation system has definitely been a good process for getting student feedback on the quality of instruction; and in that respect, it has empowered students in the sense of giving them 'voice' in our collegial evaluation of faculty performance." But, as noted above, students seem far more interested in communicating with one another regarding how to select easy instructors than in having a (surely limited) "voice" in their school's formal evaluation of instructors, indicated, among other things, by the oft-noted difficulty schools have in getting students to complete evaluations that their own peers will likely never see. Students perform work when they write evaluations, and departments feel entitled to the fruits of that work, which is, in many chairs' estimations, being foolishly squandered on RMP.

Nonetheless, several respondents are attentive to the student-as-consumer form of empowerment that motivates many RMP users: "Yes. RMP gives students who are not well-connected a way to get the local student scuttlebutt about instructors. But whether a class is easy or not, or whether a professor is hot or not, is not so important when it comes to rehiring instructors." Another chair writes: "Yes, and it also encourages 'easy grading,'" and a chair at a university in the Rocky Mountain region complains, "Yes, it empowers them to blow off steam and derail a faculty member's career when they do poorly in a course." Striking a more positive tone, another chair notes, "Yes, (thanks to RMP) both lecturers and ladder-rank faculty must place more emphasis on holding student attention, teaching at an appropriate level, and overall kindness than they otherwise would." These comments demonstrate an understanding of student empowerment that is more in line with most student responses, as they focus on ostensible improvements to the educational "product" that students consume. Situating this power within the context of consumer demand, these chairs indicate that insofar as students have economic power, reasonably organized via RMP, they can affect, directly or more likely indirectly via the threat of altering class size, the classroom, as suggested by a chair's comment that ". . . 'Rate My Professor' helps students select classes and identify faculty to avoid. Since they don't have access to other sources of information about faculty teaching, 'Rate My Professor' empowers them by giving them something to go on even if the ratings are not very accurate."

Indeed, seventeen of forty-four respondents, or 39 percent, asserted that course enrollment does affect their departments' retention of adjunct instructors.[10] A chair at a community college writes: "If there are lots of people in an adjunct class, I would suspect (the respondent's college) would want to keep them, as they provide a lot of value. When I was an adjunct at a four-year public university, large enrollments encouraged retention of adjunct instructors." A chair at a public university noted, "Enrollment size is a major consideration for retention of adjuncts. It is not the only factor but it is a primary one." And other affirmative responses include "A significant degree," "Very important," and "somewhat." Of the twenty-four respondents who wrote that course size has little or no bearing on adjunct retention, two noted that their universities do not use adjuncts and several more wrote that their schools only use adjuncts on limited bases or for large introductory courses, making it highly unlikely that an adjunct's course would not fill. The majority of negative respondents provided brief answers including "Not at all," "very little," "None at present," "None," "No effect," "A small bit," and "It does not play a major role." Nevertheless, that a significant proportion of respondents concede that course size affects adjunct retention reveals that chairs—regardless of whether or not they even look at RMP—can be indirectly affected by RMP in spite of their attitudes about that site and student preferences in general.

At the same time, chairs who deny the existence of student empowerment via RMP cling to a tenuous insistence that "Rate my Professor reviews carry no weight whatsoever." A more grounded, yet arguably naïve, assessment is offered by a chair who writes: "I think students feel empowered but unfortunately it is a false empowerment. All they are really doing is lowering their own intellectual environment and if they are truly ambitious, it will hurt them in the future. No business wants poorly educated students." Forced to acknowledge the effects of RMP, this chair can only warn students that they will suffer later in the market for their pursuit of academic sloth in the present. Representing the university's perspective, this chair fails to understand that economic prospects are bleak for most students, regardless of their scholarly accomplishments, and that they are in many ways quite skillful when it comes to the business of being a student in the here and now of the modern university.

ADJUNCTS

How then does RMP affect the most professionally vulnerable instructors at colleges and universities, adjuncts? What matters here is not the frequent insistence of numerous chairs that they "never" consult RMP, but adjuncts' *perception* of whether reviews are looked at by chairs and faculty who are in charge of hiring, rehiring, and promoting, and, beyond this perception, adjuncts' empirically grounded assumption that they will frequently not be rehired if their courses are underenrolled. Beyond the survey responses described above, there is substantial anecdotal evidence that hiring boards consult RMP reviews. An article in the *Chronicle of Higher Education* (Montell 2006) describes the rampant practice of professors and graduate students padding their reviews (the article notes, "Of the more than 50 people interviewed for this story, nearly every one had either manipulated the site or knew someone who had" [par. 13]), with one grad student confessing, "'I'm paranoid that search committees for jobs I'm up for are on RateMyProfessors right now reading my reviews'" (par. 30). The student's concern is reportedly justified, as the article goes on to recount the following story:

> A former animation instructor at a state university in Pennsylvania, who asked that her name not be used, claims that administrators fired her based mainly on some bad ratings on RateMyProfessors. Last spring, after she received a letter saying her contract would not be renewed and citing student complaints, she decided to examine her personnel file. In it she found copies of her RateMy-Professor.com reviews, with negative comments highlighted. She says her personnel file also included copies of her male colleagues' ratings from the site. She has filed a grievance. In an interview with The Chronicle, her department head insisted repeatedly that his university does not use RateMyProfessors to evaluate professors. When asked to explain the presence of those pages in her file, he said, "I don't know how they got in there." The vice president for human relations, who was present when the pages were discovered, said in an interview, "It was a mistake. She was told that it was an error, and the pages were removed." The former animation instructor isn't buying that explanation. She says, "The mistake is that they got caught. And, yes, the pages were taken out of my personnel file, but that was long after I was not renewed. It's a little late for that to be perceived as a positive action" (par. 38–40).

As with my discussion of Yelp, this study is informed by many informal conversations, in this case primarily ones that I have had with adjuncts and full-time professors mainly at the five colleges (including a prison where students did not have Internet, and thereby RMP, access) where I worked as an adjunct instructor as well as with fellow adjuncts at my grad school. It is also informed by my own experiences as an adjunct, as I have taught twenty college classes and have received numerous RMP reviews. I additionally formally surveyed forty-seven adjunct instructors who I recruited from Facebook adjunct groups throughout the country (an arguably politicized sample) and my own department's graduate student listserv. Out of forty-seven respondents forty wrote that they check their RMP reviews, which immediately illustrates a key difference between servers' relationships to Yelp and instructors' relationships to RMP. When servers check Yelp reviews of their restaurant, they do not necessarily expect to find any comments explicitly discussing them. By contrast, RMP reviews are by definition devoted to instructors, and those who are reviewed there receive, in one form or another, the entire attention of the review; the stakes are personal and high as a rule, not an exception. Instructors who check their RMP reviews therefore are also making sure that nothing libelous or embarrassing is being written about them, or, conversely, seeing if there have been any compliments written about them. This regular self-monitoring demonstrates an important difference from Yelp, as servers generally hear about good or bad Yelp reviews from managers who sometimes obsessively pore over that site. That many instructors tend to self-monitor their reviews on RMP is quite explicable but also indicates that instructors—occupying an arguably more responsible rung on the professional ladder—must pay for their relative prestige by proactively checking and to a degree internalizing their own consumerist surveillance. If they do not check the site, instructors can conceivably be at a disadvantage vis-à-vis students (and possibly colleagues and administrators) who are "in the know" about instructors' popularity, foibles, and quirks if not more harmful information.

Answering whether, and if so why, they check their reviews, respondents wrote comments including, "Yes. Always read them. They have been consistently very positive. But, a change in that would make me reevaluate my approach," "Yes, I want to know how I am perceived by students," "Yes. I care about student concerns," and "Yes, I want to learn from them." Two respondents referred to the psychological lift provided by positive reviews, with one asking whether the compliments made up for the job's paltry wages: "Yes. I usually got good reviews, and it helped boost my ego. Was that compensation for being underpaid? It actually helped, since it said that the people I was really working for appreciated my efforts. (I retired two years ago)," and "Yes, because I hope they'll say good things about me :) And if not, I hope it'll give me insight into how I could be a more effective teacher."

Describing the inevitable flipside of student compliments, numerous respondents recounted the emotional difficulty of reading insulting and sometimes malicious anonymous criticisms: "They've been harmful insofar as some students have said things that have hurt my feelings and made me self-conscious," "Sometimes they are just hurtful rather than being productive," "read evaluations once, they were mostly good but the bad ones were hard to forget," "Sometimes they seem unnecessarily harsh . . . ," "They are often harmful because they are anonymous and can be quite unfair. The last thing any poorly paid adjunct needs is to be dumped on with negativity."

One female instructor wrote: "I used to read my evals on Rate My Professor but they weren't helpful. My first reviewer posted three comments in a row and included comments like 'she has PMS 24/7' and 'She should be fired.' The long ranty stuff was removed either by the reviewer or by RMP, but the 'She should be fired' remains. Or so students tell me. . . ."

Beyond the general criticisms of RMP, there is much evidence that RMP reviews are particularly sexist. In addition to the existence of numerous cases of baldly misogynistic reviews (one instructor received a review, quickly taken down, calling her "a real bitch," although comments calling her "uptight" remain on the site), a 2015 study indicates that reviewers tend to rate male professors on a so-called intelligence scale and women professors on a so-called nurturing scale notwithstanding the fact that male and female instructors perform the same job (Huntsberry 2015). Ben Schmidt (2015) has generated an interactive word-counting chart demonstrating the consistently sexist language RMP reviewers use to describe their professors, with women being far likelier to be described as "unreasonable," "shrill," "hateful," "lovely," and "beautiful" while men are far likelier to be described as "pompous," "egotistical," and "brilliant." While one might object that RMP did not invent such sexist categories and that reviewers' biases undoubtedly preexist RMP and affect department student evaluations as well, RMP ratings' public and student audience (and, until it was eliminated, the site's explicit encouragement to rate professors' "Hotness") clearly promotes the objectification of teachers, a phenomenon that traditionally disproportionately harms women.

There is also evidence that RMP reviews discriminate against instructors, specifically Asian ones, who have accents. The author of one study, Nicholas Close Subtirelu, argues that given the rigorous English proficiency requirements placed on college and university instructors, such bias likely reflects a parochial inclination among American students to make little effort at understanding those who are racially categorized as Others, a tendency that does not apply to instructors with British accents (Subtirelu 2015; Jaschik 2015).

While RMP reviews affect different instructors in different ways, multiple respondents referred to their professional and economic interests in receiving positive student reviews, although the former respondent does not distinguish between department and RMP reviews: "Yes. A few reasons: 1) out of curiosity, 2) to see if they help me improve my teaching in any way, 3) to gauge my popularity with students which can have a range of different effects (enrollments, treatment from the department)," and "I read both kinds of reviews. My thought is that the RmP reviews are a very public face to students, the department, and potential employers, so I should be aware of what they say." Another respondent writes:

> I suspect that at one new college I work at, my supervisors have not come and observed my teaching so far (although I've worked now 9 mos there) because they are likely just going off my student evaluations (whether RmP or departmental). Please note, in some cases my supervisors are very slow to even return evaluations to me—often I have to go and ask the supervisors for them, one year later! Absolutely, overall, negative student evaluations have had a bearing on my confidence in seeking full-time employment—it is not only information that is publicly available—it's publicized as a selling point by my employers in trying to attract students to enroll. Future employers can easily access it.

Responding at length to my question on whether student evaluations in general are helpful, one respondent wrote:

> Perhaps most fundamentally, good teaching doesn't always engender comfort or easy experiences. It's not always immediately apparent to a student which

> classes or teaching styles they benefit from the most. I know this because I remember experiencing it myself as an undergraduate. Reviews can be harmful, especially RmP, because they are so unreliable, but can have a big impact. Any individual review may not have a big effect, but the overall cumulative effect of having these reviews floating around definitely creates a "consumer" mentality, which can cause teachers to second-guess their pedagogical decisions based on what reviews might say. I've seen it happen and felt that pressure myself, though I try to resist it. In the end it's something everyone feels, but that's difficult to quantify.

To a far greater degree than chairs and students, this respondent identifies the mutually antagonistic aims of student satisfaction and student learning that crystallize on RMP. Adjuncts are increasingly caught between fulfilling their professional desires to teach and the need, compounded by student reviews, to, as one respondent put it, "play to the crowd" and, as another put it, become a more "generous" grader.

In a similar vein, another respondent writes:

> Yes, and not in a good way. They have added to the drive to make higher education an infotainment industry. What students think is fun in the classroom is not necessarily what or how they should be learning. By way of example, one of my colleagues is repeatedly reviewed positively on RmP because his students note that 'he can be bribed on grades with cigarettes.'

Other adjuncts write: "Holding students to any sort of standard is seen as a bad thing to do; doing so leads you to being labeled as 'mean.' Administrators frown on this." And another writes, "Yes. I was guilty of expecting students in the final required course of an English composition to be able to read and write. This did not please my administrators."

Although many respondents acknowledged that RMP reviews could affect their job prospects, just as many respondents seemed disillusioned about those very prospects, commenting: ". . . what job prospects? Other crappy adjunct jobs? It's not like we're in line for any soon-to-be-obsolete full-time positions," "Not really, since the probability of being hired full time was very low," and "Maybe but I don't think so b/c as an adjunct I have no job prospects."

Ironically, disillusionment over poor professional prospects might have emboldened numerous respondents to adhere to professional grading guidelines in spite of departmental pressure to pass failing students, an apparent point of pride among instructors who are poorly remunerated and often treated disrespectfully by administrators and students. At the same time, the intense competition for dwindling tenure-track jobs has invested student reviews—both department and RMP—with a lose-lose quality, a phenomenon keenly recognized by several respondents: "Bad ratings kill job prospects. Good ratings don't have much effect." Other respondents noted that ratings that seem inordinately high could also draw scrutiny from department heads concerned about "pandering." And another adjunct suggested that negative student reviews might only be "scrutinized when an excuse is sought" by the department to terminate or otherwise punish the instructor, a point echoed by others. It is within this context that many adjuncts are fighting a rearguard battle to maintain grading professionalism while not scaring off students and reducing their class sizes to the point where they lose the limited work that they do have. In spite of many adjuncts' devotion to their teaching, there is enormous institutional pressure on adjuncts to make things easier on their students by passing—though not being too easy, an arbitrary standard that little reflects actual assessments of learning—undeserving students.

It is arguably because adjuncts are in the crossfire of the ongoing conflict between the competing conceptions of the modern student that respondents, to a far greater degree than students or chairs, answered the question of whether students have become empowered through reviews by referring explicitly to students becoming consumers. Respondents' answers include: "Yes, as 'consumers,'" "They believe reviews give them consumer clout. The End of Days is nigh, for higher ed, anyway," "Absolutely. Students are now customers seeking service rather than teaching."

As we have seen, student evaluations—particularly on RMP, since they, unlike most department evaluations, are read by other students—are perceived by many adjuncts to either affect or threaten to affect adjuncts' class sizes, indirectly threatening vulnerable instructors' job security. Similarly, negative reviews—or even overly positive ones asserting that the instructor is extremely "easy"—are perceived by numerous adjuncts as playing a role in their employment prospects.

WHAT KIND OF POWER?

Although most department chairs, more so than in the case of restaurant managers and Yelp, assert that they do not consult RMP, RMP has affected the ways some instructors teach, a point not only expressed by some of my respondents—"poor grades lead to poor evals"—but also by recent research demonstrating the relationship between RMP and grade inflation (Stroebe, 2016). I myself have been made keenly aware of the pressures that RMP introduces into teaching, a point that ironically can be elaborated by examining two somewhat banal reviews that I have received. After I finished teaching a U.S. government course at City College in New York, I was pleased to receive a complimentary if terse review describing me as a "good guy." While this review likely referred to my flexibility as an instructor (e.g., I have often been lenient when it comes to permitting students to make up exams), it also conveyed, as I saw it, a sense of a "reasonable," "down to earth," "regular guy" who cared about his students. As with my other RMP reviews, I spent some time thinking about which student wrote the review, and I guessed that it was a young man who I would sometimes chat with before class. In spite of, or possibly in part because of, the implicit sexism of this description (a woman, by definition, cannot be a "good guy"), I positively viewed myself through my student's eyes as well as, critically, through the eyes of everyone else who might come across the review, and on some level I decided to commit myself to being this reasonable, amiable, "good guy." Teaching, to a degree, is performing, and I was presented with public feedback that articulated one potential role to choose from—one that, notably, was well received by at least one member of the audience.

By contrast, following a course entitled Genocide and Film that I designed and taught at a performing arts college on the Upper East Side of Manhattan, I received a negative review that described me as "boring" (and also complained that I was "kind of a tough grader"). Again, after thinking about who might have written it, I anticipated the reactions of future potential students who would read the review. Considering the review, I reflected on my lectures and thought about strategies for being more engaging and animated, but I also thought about the content of my lectures, specifically the difficulty of some of the concepts I was introducing. There is only so much one could do to not be abstract and theoretical, i.e., for many, "boring," without abandoning core instructional goals. Insofar as I have been successful in improving my teaching following this review, I can credit RMP. However, such improvement, such as it exists, did not primarily reflect a concern with pedagogical efficacy per se. I had in fact, possibly self-servingly, guessed that the reviewer was a particularly anti-intellectual young woman who was unreceptive and at times hostile to the course's major themes. That is, I was less concerned with more effectively teaching students than with making sure that I did not lose students through boring them, a distinction that gives me considerable consternation. In fact, this approach resembles the so-called lowest common denominator strategy of much of the entertainment industry, in which the attempt to generate the broadest possible market share—alienating none at "the bottom"—leads increasingly to the production of unchallenging products that comfortably meet and leave consumers where they are: the very opposite of effective teaching. As I am presently preparing to begin a full-time, tenure track position, it has occurred to me that I will now have a more secure position from which to increase my rigor and further challenge my students, even if doing so risks "boring" and losing some of them. Irrespective of my popularity, I will have guaranteed courses the following semester for the duration of my contract, as opposed to the semester-to-semester work I performed as an adjunct. However, accepting the possibility of further alienating uninterested students in order to provide a superior experience for the more motivated ones assumes that I will be able to easily jettison my many hours of self-conditioning as an adjunct, which has been influenced in part by my desire to entertain students if only in order to ensure that I would continue to be able to have new ones.

In this chapter I have argued that RMP has harnessed students' collective power in changing—even if indirectly via affecting course size—the ways that some courses are taught. As universities and colleges increasingly rely on adjunct employment, the power of online student reviewers will arguably only increase. Yet, as with Yelp, we should ask what kind of power is generated through RMP. On one hand, student reviewers produce enormous wealth for RMP through writing and posting the unpaid reviews that are the basis of that site's online traffic and advertising revenue. This unpaid work can be viewed as the fare reviewers must pay in order to amplify their voices on RMP's mass platform. On the other hand, reviewers derive a sense of power, enjoyment, and satisfaction from participating on the site. Students, as with Yelp reviewers and servers, experience power in taking putatively shoddy instructors to task or, alternately, in setting the record straight by defending unfairly reviled instructors. Students also take their reviews seriously and adhere to formal and informal guidelines centered around fairness, honesty, duty, and conscientiousness. Indeed, RMP, like Yelp, provides users with a community of like-minded users devoted to common goals, harnessing users' senses of social cooperation and altruism. However, it is significant that such cooperation and altruism are generated through evaluations of an external subject in the form of workers. That is, the solidarity that both RMP and Yelp inculcate is produced through the reification of consumerist identities and goals. Notably, these goals—implicitly structured by capitalist institutions and explicitly articulated on reviewer sites—are poorly equipped to advance consumers' economic interests or, arguably, the broader interests of human society. In the case of Yelp, reviews undoubtedly affect some small restaurants, but they do not affect the restaurant industry—including the prices consumers pay—as such. In the case of RMP, reviews are neither designed nor equipped to challenge the costs of tuition and are thereby incapable, for instance, of ameliorating crippling student debt. In both cases, reviewer empowerment is highly circumscribed. That RMP and Yelp users empower themselves primarily through monitoring, evaluating, and disciplining workers suggests not only the contingency and relative weakness of consumer power but also some of the ways in which contemporary capitalism channels desires for community and individual agency toward externalized profit production created, in the final analysis, at the expense of workers.

NOTES

1. Sections of this chapter were previously published in *New Labor Forum* (2018).

2. RMP has added a section in which students can also review their schools, but the page devoted to instructor evaluations is still discrete and the main draw of the site.

3. RMP changed its ratings criteria in May 2016, replacing "clarity," "helpfulness," and "easiness" with "overall quality" and "difficulty." RMP told me that they instituted these changes "after receiving feedback from students."

4. Epstein's article, "Hotness and Quality" (2006), begins, "If you're not sexy, you might want to be easy."

5. According to Otto, Sanford, and Ross (2008), "It may be argued that data from these sites are characterized by bias such as instructors' personality, charisma and grading leniency, and are therefore not of value as a measure for either faculty performance or student learning (see Cashin 1996, 1999; Greenwald and Gilmore 1997; Wilson 1998; Liaw and Goh 2003). In fact, this interpretation is most common among the faculty we meet" (355).

6. Tenured professors have in fact told me that student evaluations are typically ignored by their chairs unless a nonstudent related conflict arises; only then do negative student evaluations suddenly attract concern from instructors' superiors.

7. To be sure, participation in some activities, such as the movement to Boycott, Divest, and Sanction (BDS) Israel, has led to punitive action by administrations against both students and professors.

8. Whenever possible, I emailed departments of history, political science, sociology, anthropology, English, physics, biology, art history, business (economics), and computer science.

9. Among other possibilities, such vehemence could reflect the fact that large universities frequently hire adjuncts from graduate students whom chairs personally know and have already in effect vetted.

10. In a follow-up Survey Monkey survey emailed to prior survey respondents, I asked chairs, *To what degree, if any, does course enrollment size influence the retention, promotion, or termination of adjunct instructors?*

Chapter Five

Conclusion

It is a notorious mistake to suppose that there exists a natural human subjectivity, in which in our relationship with present conditions we have deviated from some imaginary human essence. On the contrary, human subjectivity is an effect of its interaction with specific historic material conditions and is thereby always not only evolving but also expressing, in a multitude of ways, the systemic forces that substantially structure and influence it. As political-economic institutions have become more powerful, technologically sophisticated, and intrusive, human subjectivity—for all its variation—has reflected among other things the changing imperatives and techniques through which it develops.

In an earlier stage of capitalism, a newly entrenched division of labor helped produce competing, if not contradictory, subjectivities in the forms of, among other identities, worker and consumer. Amid the decline of labor consciousness (brought about in part through the demise of unionization) and the evolution of consumer consciousness, the current postindustrial service or neoliberal economy has helped produce a more internally consistent, if not yet hegemonic, subjectivity reflecting what we might describe as the marketized subject. This highly individualized, or entrepreneurial, subject does not simply express the economic utilitarianism and self-serving rationality caricaturized in the traditional image of economic man, in which the logic and values of the ascending economic order had been *internalized* by the individual. Instead, the self-governance of today's marketized subject is a means for *collective governance*, in which all other economic actors—that is, ultimately, everyone—are subjected to the logic, values, and demands of inviolable market principles: a secular, if not totalitarian, religion. It is thereby unsurprising that some of the most common utterances regarding service workers are variations of the refrain: "If she does not like it, she should get another job."

Notably, the emergence of an increasingly "boundary-less" marketized subject has not diminished expressions of human solidarity. It has, however, applied human solidarity to its own purposes, as consumer managers collectively evaluate external antagonists through the application of values such as efficiency and courteousness. As we have seen, online reviewers, more than anything else, seek to "help" their fellow users. Invoking the maxim of "paying it forward," reviewers reference debts they seek to repay to those who have helped them. Some users refer to wanting to spare others the terrible experiences that they endured, or alternately their desire to share their positive experiences with others. Simultaneously, some reviewers express a fidelity to an informal "code" based on their website's formal and informal practices, in which they feel duty-bound to treat their reviews with seriousness and conscientiousness lest they tarnish their community's and their own reputations. Respondents on both Yelp and RMP scoffed at suggestions that they might write dishonest reviews or put personal gain in front of their obligations to impartiality. In the case of Yelp, where reviewers use recognizable names and build reputations, abusing the system or otherwise violating "the code" can also lead reviewers to lose their frequently coveted "Elite" status. In the case of RMP, reviewers, who are wholly anonymous, have noted that abusing the site—for instance through threatening an instructor with a negative review—would not only be counterproductive from a practical perspective but would undermine reviewers' carefully maintained sense of integrity.

To be sure, many reviewers are also motivated by conventional self-interest. Yelp reviewers have noted that they enjoy receiving "likes" or compliments on their posts, and many reviewers additionally take pride in their "Elite" status and enjoy the benefits—such as party invitations and free food—it confers. A few Yelp reviewers have even expressed a desire to use their Yelp reviews as a platform to launch careers as food critics. Yelp reviewers also find it gratifying to not only "call out" unpleasant restaurants and servers but also to "reward" small and obscure restaurants that they have taken a liking to. RMP reviewers, largely in pursuit of easy graders, knowingly amplify the traditional "word of mouth" that informs fellow students about desirable and undesirable instructors.

That is, the personal rewards that come from being a member of a reviewer community, contributing to an effort larger than themselves through helping others, are interwoven with the feelings of power that such activity provides. Yelp and RMP reviewers recognize that they have power, and, while they insist that they use their power responsibly, numerous respondents simultaneously reveal that such power nevertheless gives them personal gratification. Several reviewers describe the thrill of playing the expert, for instance, concealing that they are a Yelp reviewer and dining "just like any other individual" in order to experience restaurants in a "more exciting" manner. Another reviewer remarks that he does not write reviews for the "fame" but in order to "let people know there are good people in the world," that is, in order to demonstrate his goodness to an audience.

Reviewers also recognize that reviews can indirectly influence restaurants and instructors through affecting restaurant patronage and class sizes, respectively. Yet there is a frequent disconnect between the expectations that reviewers have for their reviews and the impact reviews often have on workplaces. Most reviewers are far more concerned with their interactions with other consumers than with the effects of their reviews on either restaurant servers or college and university instructors. Nearly all of my Yelp respondents did not know of any cases of servers being terminated due to negative Yelp reviews, while most of my RMP respondents doubted whether instructors take any notice of reviews.

Reflecting more an ultimate lack of concern than willful denial, reviewers' emphasis on the interests of fellow users at the expense of workers nonetheless indicates what we might term the wages of Yelping. That is, while constituting a mutually supportive community, online consumer reviewers do not *transcend* the competitive antagonisms of capitalist social relations but instead export them from the site of the individual to that of a collective that, in the case of Yelp, derives its purpose from putatively challenging or rewarding businesses. In fact, as we have seen, the efforts of such organized consumer power are frequently appropriated by business and directed first and foremost against workers. Whereas Yelp can undoubtedly harm individual businesses, it does not challenge the *system* of business, or capitalism, itself. As such, it does not interrupt business's ability or need to extract value through exploiting the labor supply. On the contrary, Yelp reinforces this exploitation indirectly through intensifying competition among restaurants and directly through intensifying competition among workers who face the brunt of Yelp discipline as mediated through management. By contrast, RMP does not highlight criticism of businesses at all and instead focuses on workers, professionals who can be seen as businesses unto themselves, some of whom can theoretically "go out of business" due to repeated negative reviews.

In its zeal to help fellow consumers and manage workers, the marketized subject as expressed through online consumer managers has had mixed effects on professional management, which has greeted the former with ambivalence. There are of course, as we have seen above, important differences in the ways online reviews affect restaurants and schools. Small restaurants are far more vulnerable to Yelp reviews than are large restaurants, and chain spokespeople tend to discuss Yelp in a more positive manner than do managers at small restaurants. Indeed, managers at small restaurants are sometimes openly hostile to Yelp and its perceived facilitation of customer encroachment into management's field of expertise. Nevertheless, these managers routinely scour Yelp reviews and incorporate elements of reviews into their management of their servers as they see fit.

Managerial techniques in using reviews vary. For instance, some managers hold formal weekly meetings to discuss Yelp reviews, celebrating good reviews, while other managers restrict their Yelp-based interaction with employees to one-on-one discussions in passing. Yet, regardless of managerial style, Yelp has been invoked to praise, reprimand, and terminate workers. In nearly all cases management consistently acts on complaints and compliments about servers, though even these complaints and compliments are selectively invoked. As we saw, a server was reprimanded after a Yelp reviewer praised the server for his detailed knowledge of opera, revealing, presumably unbeknownst to the reviewer, that the server was spending too much time with one customer. Notably, managers do not tend to be concerned about reviewers who complain of being "chased" from their tables. That is, management's response to reviewers' service complaints is itself selective, although management readily invokes the mantra of customer satisfaction as a tool to motivate and discipline employees. Such appeals to the sovereign consumer can function to exonerate management from blame when disciplining workers—since such punishment is ostensibly "out of their hands"—and generate solidarity between management and workers against a supposedly all-powerful common enemy in the form of the customer (Fuller and Smith 1991). In other words, managers can be said to appropriate Yelp reviews for purposes that may overlap with but are ultimately distinct from and at times at odds with consumer interests.

At the same time, managers generally subordinate or ignore consumer complaints about food and prices. There are exceptions, such as a restaurant in Cambria, California, whose employees told me that the owner has in fact lowered prices on some dishes after multiple Yelp complaints. This is a restaurant whose customers are divided between town locals and Cambria's numerous tourists, suggesting that the restaurant may have alienated the former by exorbitant charges aimed at the latter. Nevertheless, this restaurant's willingness to lower prices due to complaints on Yelp is an exception seemingly proving the rule. Numerous managers and owners have dismissed the suggestion that they ought to adjust their prices or menu due to demands posted on Yelp. As one manager noted, customers who are unsatisfied by what they find on the menu "can go to another restaurant." Restaurants, particularly in New York City where I conducted most of my research, operate in an intensely competitive environment, and many are undoubtedly unable to lower prices lest they risk going out of business. It also seems likely, however, that managers simply resent, as in the case of reviewers' food recommendations, being told what to do by those who lack, as managers see it, their training and expertise. By contrast, customers' and managers' desire for "good service" is more aligned, although, as noted, customers and managers do not always agree on its definition.

While restaurant managers maintain an ambivalent relationship with Yelp, department chairs frequently insist that they have no relationship at all with RMP. Department chairs across disciplines in the social sciences, natural sciences, and humanities in predominantly liberal arts colleges and public universities express disdain for RMP and frequently vehemently deny that they use the site in their evaluations of instructors. Such vehemence by itself can indicate that chairs, who are academics themselves, are affronted by the mere suggestion that they would incorporate a website known for its unregulated and ostensibly unreliable content into their professional evaluations of employees. Indeed, numerous chairs referred to RMP's putative selection-bias among other alleged problems with the site.

However, other chairs, in guarded and qualified language, conceded that they do occasionally and "informally" "glance" at RMP when reviewing a potential hire, or that they know that other members of the hiring committee look at the site. There is a third, albeit small, category of responses, made exclusively by chairs at community colleges. These respondents openly admit to relying on RMP when evaluating adjuncts. Based on these three response types, I have suggested that chairs at noncommunity colleges view RMP as a disreputable foe in a turf war over influence on department hiring, rehiring, and promotion of adjunct instructors in particular and the university in general. I posit that community college chairs are likelier to openly consult RMP in part because community colleges are typically accorded less prestige than liberals arts colleges and universities, and community college chairs are thereby less likely to feel compelled to protect their schools' reputations from being tarnished by open association with RMP. Relatedly, community colleges generally function with more limited budgets than that of other schools and, with higher proportions of working-class students, who frequently go into trades, are frequently more integrated into market culture than are elite universities. Due to the reduced availability of public funding, it is additionally possible that chairs incorporate RMP into their hiring decisions as a matter of material resourcefulness, a consideration that would hardly apply to generously endowed schools.

Chairs who do not use RMP note repeatedly that students already have a voice in their departments' hiring decisions through department-provided student evaluations, which, according to some chairs, are freer of the selection bias allegedly plaguing RMP. Yet, students are typically not privy to what other students write in department-provided evaluations. By contrast, RMP bypasses departments altogether and enables students to communicate directly with one another. Accordingly, RMP reviews are designed to reflect what students, rather than departments, are likeliest to find relevant about instructors.

Notwithstanding its claims of naturalness, inevitability, or apolitical rationality, the marketized subject takes as its ultimate antagonist—in effect if not always intent—wage laborers. Although it is tempting to doubt the significance of online reviews by noting that employment is at-will and that workers can be fired at any time, the significance of online review sites lays less in the fact that workers are being terminated due to negative reviews than in the fact that the workers who are not fired have been made keenly aware that they are now being potentially monitored and reported on by any and all customers or students—that workers, in other words, are more concretely *fireable* due to negative reviews (De Genova 2005). Servers I spoke with reported that they are cognizant of the fact that anyone can be a Yelp reviewer, and that this awareness has led them to be more "considerate" and "work harder," and that they feel "more pressure to perform" because of Yelp, which "definitely adds stress." In this regard, Yelp, constituting consumer-driven austerity, has helped accelerate a mass and permanent "speed-up" that has increased worker productivity amid continuing glut and long-term reduced growth.

The disciplinary effect of Yelp resembles the way in which RMP affects adjunct instructors. In this case, workers' employers typically deny consulting RMP, in contrast to restaurant managers who openly admit to consulting Yelp. Yet what is significant is not whether chairs in fact consult RMP when hiring, rehiring, or promoting adjuncts, but adjuncts' general *perception* that chairs do so. Moreover, even if chairs ignore RMP, they typically do not ignore adjuncts' class sizes, which can be directly influenced by RMP reviews. Over 80 percent of my respondents read their reviews on RMP, with some explicitly noting that they read reviews because they are concerned about their enrollment sizes. One respondent noted that the awareness of reviews can lead adjuncts to "second-guess their pedagogical decisions based on what reviews might say," while another remarked that "poor grades lead to poor evals" and that the fear of negative evaluations has made the instructor a more "generous" grader. Another respondent noted that reviews have encouraged adjuncts to "play to the crowd," a sentiment I have encountered not only in exchanges with colleagues but also in my considerations of my own teaching. The fact that some adjuncts have told me that they refuse to look at RMP due to their fear of being influenced by reviews, as if siren songs, further attests to the influence of that site.

While servers typically learn about their Yelp reviews through managers, adjuncts typically discover their RMP reviews themselves. Indeed, the latter are explicitly devoted to individually named instructors, which helps explain why so many adjuncts read their reviews. I argue that adjuncts, through monitoring their own RMP reviews without a managerial intermediary, to a greater degree than restaurant workers are susceptible to internalizing consumer standards as their own. To some extent, the need for self-management and initiative is characteristic of middle-level and upper-level professionals in general. Yet even such self-management is generally prompted by and mediated through superiors. The case of RMP is distinct insofar as adjuncts' self-management is prompted directly by students themselves.

Additionally, there is a fundamental bias in reviewing to which workers are uniquely susceptible. Yelp reviewers demand that service be efficient and attentive—some reviewers even demand that they be made to feel "important and valued"—which servers for a variety of reasons are not always able to do. Servers have finite time and energy and making one customer feel "important and valued" can therefore come at the expense of comparatively neglecting others. This empirical basis of customer reviews particularly harms workers—who are typically more visible to customers than are managers or owners—insofar as reviewers cannot necessarily see that a manager cut floor staff or that a cook called in sick or simply that, by definition, not everyone can be treated as if they were "important and valued." Similarly, students are not always aware of the department requirements—including minimum standards on assigned readings—that instructors must adopt, nor the often high number of courses adjuncts must teach, spreading themselves thin in order to fulfill their often onerous financial obligations.

As opposed to restaurant workers, however, adjuncts do take their work home with them and are therefore at times capable, for instance, of meeting reviewers' demands by grading papers more quickly and attentively. Yet, more than any other aim, RMP reviewers seek "easy"—or the euphemistic "fair"—grades, often presenting adjuncts with contradictory interests in either providing good grades in order to maintain or increase enrollment or providing stringent grades in order to maintain personal and professional standards. Yelp reviews, by contrast, do not make demands on servers to alter their judgements as such, although the demand to perform the "emotional labor" of smiling when one does not feel up to it can take a toll of its own (Hochschild 2003 [1983]). To be sure, different adjuncts have been criticized by departments for both grading too easily and too harshly, indicating that department grading standards can, depending on the department and school, either be aligned with RMP reviewers' demands or in conflict with them.

While wage labor is frequently alienating and exploitative, historically workers can and do make efforts to reduce, if not necessarily the material alienation embedded in disparate property relations, the psychological alienation of performing labor under someone else's control. For instance, restaurant workers can entertain themselves with their smartphones during lulls, temporarily forgetting the fact that they might rather be relaxing at home or hanging out with friends. Yelp has made such "time theft" far more difficult, as it is easier—and safer, if customers fear retaliation from workers—for customers to "out" workers on Yelp than it is to find a manager to complain to in person. The pre-Internet direct confrontations between workers and aggrieved service recipients could undoubtedly be hostile and unpleasant, but workers nonetheless often maintained some leverage in these encounters, insofar as, for instance, service-recipients were dependent on workers to fulfill their "real-time" demands (Leidner 1993). For example, workers could withhold charm and helpfulness or can "accidentally" retaliate against difficult customers by, for instance, spilling drinks on them (Hochschild 2003 [1983], 114; Leidner 1993, 41). Online consumer management is not only anonymous but also retroactive. Although reviewers write to "warn others" about unhappy experiences, negative reviews targeting workers can simultaneously function as revenge, moving customer-worker antagonisms from direct even if unequal confrontations to unilateral assaults on workers that the latter is inadequately equipped to respond to.

At the same time, restaurant workers, the most vulnerable member of the worker-consumer-employer triad, lack the leverage to conduct Yelp "boycotts" or attempt other managerial strategies to subvert Yelp's power.[1] To be sure, servers can encourage quid pro quos by providing customers with complimentary or generous items, for instance, in exchange for good reviews. Nevertheless, such efforts represent individual, or guerrilla, acts that are more vulnerable to backfire and are, unlike managerial strategies, unorganized, indicating again that the demands of management and the demands of customers are not one and the same notwithstanding paeans to the sovereign customer. Adjunct instructors, even more so, struggle to manipulate RMP to their own ends, even if they can write favorable reviews of themselves. While a server who provides a customer with a free drink may very well go unnoticed by management, adjuncts who attempt to "buy off" students with high grades or pandering instruction will likely be called to the attention of chairs or deans concerned about excessive grade inflation. Whereas restaurant servers have reported working harder and being more attentive due to their awareness of Yelp, the professional demands of adjunct instructors are more fundamentally in conflict with the demands of RMP reviewers who prioritize "ease" above all. RMP reviewers rarely demand to be taught better in the manner that Yelp reviewers demand to be served better. This discrepancy illustrates a contradiction characterizing higher education. Restaurants typically make no claims to be anything other than quintessential service businesses, while colleges and universities are historically and in their ideal form insulated from market forces. This is clearly not the case, although department chairs do not always appear to have fully grasped this fact, specifically as it pertains to student-cum-consumer empowerment via RMP.

A major theme of this book has been that online consumer management should be understood as being both exploitative and alienating. Again, such a statement immediately appears counterintuitive since reviewers frequently derive considerable enjoyment from their participation on review sites. Yet, as we have seen, prosumers in general help produce considerable revenue for Web 2.0 platforms. With every comment, photo, or status update these platforms expand their content and potential readership. These are in effect consumer-run websites that would cease to exist without the millions of unpaid contributions that attract visitor traffic and thereby enable site owners to increase advertising rates. Through describing their various preferences and tendencies, prosumers additionally furnish personal data that can be analyzed and sold for the further enrichment of platform owners. Because the psychological rewards that prosumers receive for their efforts function as a wage, albeit a virtual one that arguably does not reflect the massive monetary value such efforts produce, it is tempting to identify online consumer management as a form of wage labor. Following Marx, this book has argued that such work does not in itself constitute wage labor, does not generate surplus value, and should accordingly not be viewed as exploitation in this formal sense.

However, as opposed to other forms of prosumption, online consumer management, through increasing the productivity of *actual* wage laborers (e.g., paid employees such as servers), can in fact enhance worker productivity and surplus value and thereby overall economic growth. In this regard online consumer management is unique. While instances in which online consumer management has increased worker productivity are difficult to quantify, the practice can nonetheless potentially grow and become more systematic. Indeed, since the 1973 global economic downturn, neoliberal policies—or, following Foucault, what we might call marketized governance—have radically cut business costs, not least by slashing middle management. Management, after all, has been historically necessary to supervise wage workers but in itself does not produce profit. There therefore exist powerful incentives to reduce or replace management as an unprofitable cost of business, provided that wage workers can be made to productively work on their own or under the direction of other, unpaid, actors. The emergence of online consumer management presents a potentially invaluable tool with which to pursue this goal.

Online consumer management should simultaneously be understood as alienating. Again, this initially sounds curious, since we have seen the ways in which online consumer management, and prosumption in general, can in fact reduce the psychological alienation, or ennui, of users. Respondents take reviewing seriously and find personal value in it. Finding fulfillment in being a member of a community, reviewers enthusiastically give back to that community, characterizing reviewer activity as an apparent form of social reciprocity based on fairness, honesty, and helpfulness. There is undoubtedly therapeutic value in reaching others, telling them something useful that they did not know, and listening to their experiences, perceptions, and advice in return. While it is often impractical for us to regularly meet with one another out in the world, the Internet has enabled us to do so virtually, on our own time and from our own homes.

We should accordingly be highly suspect of descriptions of "false consciousness" or other notions of dupery that simplify and dismiss the complex and frequently gratifying relationships people have with the Internet, which has become integral not only for work but also for the social interaction that we might say defines our very "species being." Facebook is emblematic in this regard, as it is one of the easiest ways for geographically dispersed family members and friends to keep in touch with one another. Merely sharing family photos and "likes" can provide users with feelings of connection, continuity, and rootedness amid an often isolated social existence. We do not, however, want to be too hasty in congratulating capitalism for providing technologies that help people meet their needs and desires insofar as it was that same political-economic system—through dislocating communities and shrinking families while simultaneously placing enormous burdens on them—that helped introduce modern alienation in the first place. Whereas social media such as Facebook and Twitter facilitate communal—indeed global—interaction and thereby reduce psychological alienation, they simultaneously reproduce another form of, material, alienation that is embedded in capitalist property relations themselves.

The online platforms that enable much contemporary social interaction are not an atavism of a distant commons but are instead massive, hierarchically controlled, capitalist enterprises. Facebook users have little influence over a web layout that is designed to direct, i.e., manipulate, users' activity, first and foremost by keeping them *on* the site and thereby exposed to advertisers and data extraction in service to astronomical profit. It is not by accident that the red (a "trigger colour") notification alert in the upper right-hand corner of a Facebook page is nearly impossible to ignore, as its signification of potential rewards produces the same addictive endorphin rush experienced by compulsive gamblers (Lewis 2017). Indeed, Facebook and other social media can be likened in other ways to a casino, one in which the mirrors are now selfies and the liquor takes the form of likes.

Users who have to rely on social media for rewarding interaction at the end—or in the midst—of a hectic day simultaneously have to cope with occasional terms of service and web design updates. It is evidence of ultimate weakness that users have to adapt to new, and unilaterally administered and frequently awkward, layouts and features. Even redesigns, as with Yelp's 2005 reboot, that are *inspired* by users' preferences reflect a primacy of profit, the condition under which all other decisions are evaluated. Users on Snapchat were in fact so frustrated with the introduction of changes to that site that over one million of them signed a petition demanding that Snapchat revert to its previous layout (Griffin 2018). Notably, Snapchat has refused to abandon the updates, reminding users that, notwithstanding the time and energy they spend on the site and the value they bring to it, it is not *their* site after all and that user preferences are, in the final analysis, accommodated only when they are in line with the demands of profit. Additionally, online platforms including Facebook and Twitter regularly suspend users for political speech that violates those sites' often opaque guidelines. Whereas social media sites are assuredly interested in profit, such political regulation indicates that profit maximization is never a purely economic affair. Rather, having fulfilled (or exploited) the social needs of its users by ameliorating their psychological alienation, such sites must nevertheless ensure that they do not wholly *eliminate* the causes of alienation or enable autonomous users to transcend their dependency on social media's for-profit "cure." Such sites have both the desire and capacity to ensure that users do not, among other things, cultivate a significant political project that would existentially threaten capitalism and thereby these sites' existence itself.

As we have seen, the contradictory dynamic in which the amelioration of psychological alienation is offset by the intensification of material alienation characterizes Yelp and RMP as well. Users on both sites experience the gratification of cooperative and helpful activity that is rewarded by likes and other forms of public appreciation. That numerous reviewers appear to develop feelings of empowerment though their interactions with these sites can be interpreted as an indication that users experience a lack of power in their ordinary lives. Such activity—the enjoyment of pretending that you are not a Yelp reviewer and are instead "just like any other individual" because "it's more exciting that way!"—appears compensatory and evokes among other things the contemporary cultural obsession with super heroes, that is, seemingly normal people who in fact possess a secret and awesome power. Yet, irrespective of such feelings of shared purpose and power, Yelp users are dependent on the rules and guidelines of that platform and can, for instance, lose their Elite status if they slacken their rate of reviews. We can only imagine the sense of dismay and loss that would arise among many "Elite" reviewers if Yelp were to be, for one reason or another, shut down. More broadly, online reviewing, notwithstanding reviewers' personal rewards, increases the profitability of large capitalist organizations that are part and parcel of the political-economic order that helps produce and maintain contemporary alienation in the first place.

There is also little indication that Yelp, notwithstanding its arguable effects on worker productivity, improves consumers' overall experiences or power. Rating systems are fundamentally comparative. By design, not every restaurant can receive a perfect rating, or else the rating system would have no meaning. While one might argue that online rating systems can pressure restaurants to exponentially improve via a "race to the top," such abstractions are not consistent with present-day business realities. Restaurants cannot exponentially improve service insofar as they have finite resources that must be carefully allocated in competition with rivals. That is, unless restaurants are capable of pricing out general customers and focusing on elite, highly affluent clienteles in necessarily limited markets, restaurants will continue to have an interest in reducing costs through purchasing suboptimal foods and understaffing shifts while increasing profit through chasing tables. In that regard, most restaurants will continue to have a structural interest in providing not only "good service" but also "poor service."[2]

RMP, however, evinces, more so than Yelp, consumer power. Instructors, in contrast to the server-customer relationship, have significant power over students, whom they evaluate and grade. Significantly, student empowerment through RMP has come into being through the ongoing transformation of the historic teacher-student relationship. We need not idealize this historic relationship—which was prone to abuse and unfairness—to note that its transformation into a service provider-recipient relationship brings into question the nature of education itself. Critical, sometimes unkind, scrutiny is arguably irreconcilable with the passivity and indulgence associated with service provision. Yet this is no paternalistic or sentimental concern. The department chair who warned that students would pay a price for their pursuit of easy courses via RMP was correct but not in the way that she believed. Students will not be worthless to the economy because they were not good students who cultivated their intellectual faculties, but because the ease with which they can acquire their grades and degrees merely reflects their relative lack of worth in the contemporary marketplace. The greater availability and concomitant commercialization of higher education have predictably come at the price of inflationary degrees that have not only lost their status as elite signifiers but also represent, for most students, long-term indebtedness. RMP has helped turn students into consumers but not powerful actors in the modern university.

The intensification of workers' exploitation and alienation through online consumer management has important consequences. As oft noted, U.S. economic policy since the 1970s has transformed from subsidizing manufacturing to establishing the conditions for the expansion of the service sector and—through what Srnicek has labeled asset-price Keynesianism (e.g., loose monetary policy)—ultimately today's tech industry (Srnicek 2017). This fundamental structural shift has produced greater long-term unemployment (and underemployment) and the growing use of precarious, often temporary, "just-in-time" work devoid of benefits or any semblance of security. This restructuring has dramatically increased pressure on not only the unemployed but also on those who do have jobs, as wages for workers have stagnated since the 1970s, savings have gone down, and debt has skyrocketed as credit cards have moved into supplement workers' reduced income. It is within this context, exacerbated by the enduring effects of the 2008 crash, that workers have become vulnerable to online consumer management. While it is not new that workers are being monitored and reported on by consumers, the extent and degree to which they currently are is in fact unprecedented.

Considering recent history and our ongoing economic and political conditions, it is not difficult to speculate on the future implications of online consumer management. Although service work is low-paying and often unpleasant, one of its traditional advantages is that, unlike many office jobs, you do not have to take your work home with you. However, with workers' increased vulnerability and consumers' ability to publicly complain about any aspect of an employee's manner or appearance, workers can feel pressured to spend parts of their "free time" working on "improving their personality," for instance through developing strategies for managing difficult customers with a positive attitude—lessons one can glean from "self-help" literature. Employees working with the public can also feel further pressured to obsess over their appearance, for instance by going to the gym more often or even conceivably undergoing cosmetic surgery in order to remain competitive in an industry in which it is standard procedure to employ conventionally attractive people. While the notion of obtaining cosmetic surgery in order to keep one's job might seem farfetched, we should remember that actors and actresses, derided as superficial, have long done so in order to protect their livelihoods. Even if servers do not go to such lengths, we can imagine scenarios in which they might think twice about attending a party the night before a morning shift so that they can appear fresh and alert for customers, a prudence that would be reasonable for airplane pilots but not necessarily for those whose job involves delivering pancakes, eggs, and coffee.

Ironically, it is on RMP rather than Yelp where workers are frequently judged on their appearance. We have seen adjuncts complain that reviews have "hurt . . . feelings and made (them) self-conscious," "were hard to forget," and were sometimes "unnecessarily harsh." While such concerns need not express anxieties about personal attractiveness per se, they do in fact express anxiety. Specifically, public monitoring of precarious employees—viewed not only by students but also, many adjuncts assume, by chairs and possibly even potential employers—can function to alienate adjuncts from their own sense of professional competence, skill, and values. RMP reviews cause some teachers to "second-guess their pedagogical decisions. . . . I've seen it happen and felt that pressure myself, though I try to resist it. In the end it's something everyone feels, but that's difficult to quantify." Such pressure to "play to the crowd" can also have political consequences. Acknowledging that RMP can affect the *content* of teaching and classroom discussions, particularly for adjuncts, Eva Swidler asks, "What vulnerable professor wants to raise an issue that might anger even only a vocal and aggressive 5 percent of students? Any adjunct knows that all you need for a lousy showing on a ratings site is a handful of angry trolls sitting in the back row of class, getting resentful about class time spent on a topic they disdain" (Swidler 2018). In an era of increasing political polarization, intolerance, and public scandals often resulting in the punishment of subversive academics, playing to the RMP crowd can very well result in increased self-censorship and intellectual homogeneity.

Although capitalism tends to deskill labor in order to reduce costs and increase managerial leverage, there have been historic obstacles to deskilling. As we have seen with service work, it is counterproductive for managers to direct workers with too heavy a hand since effective service work is characterized by the spontaneity, creativity, and responsiveness that generally come from relatively organic and unhindered social interactions (Fuller and Smith 1991). Accordingly, managers, particularly since the 1970s, have incorporated customers into the production process as informal, and unpaid, managers, a process that has exponentially expanded through Yelp. Management has had a particularly difficult time deskilling employees in the professional classes given the substantial expertise such workers must accumulate in order to qualify for such work in the first place. Indeed, "deskilled professionals" sounds like a contradiction in terms. Management has had, however, much success in reducing the value, if not always the skills, of numerous professional workers. Universities and colleges, for instance, have for decades increasingly staffed adjunct instructors not with PhDs but with graduate students working for reduced wages and no benefits (Powelson 2011). It was not, however, until market mechanisms, in the form of student reviewers, began to oversee aspects of instructor management that adjunct instructors began being deskilled. Whereas chairs and administrators initially controlled this process through the internal implementation and evaluation of department-issued student assessments, schools have lost some control over this process through the expansion of external student-based websites such as RMP. Although most department chairs—save those at more market-oriented community colleges—resent the potential reduction of their control over employees, the *effects* of such external control are nonetheless congruent with schools' general aim of establishing leverage over labor. In this regard, RMP users are doing department chairs and administrators' work for them. While adjuncts today possess enormous knowledge based on their advanced graduate studies, RMP—which rewards ease, entertainment value, and attractiveness—currently threatens to deskill adjuncts through undermining not instructors' knowledge base but their pedagogical freedom and thereby experience and expertise (Powelson 2011). It is not difficult to imagine a future in which a more regulated version of RMP—for instance, devoid of bogus accounts—can, through the mechanism of altering course sizes, adopt increased responsibility for managing, that is, controlling, adjuncts.

Consumers have always been accorded a subordinate position within capitalism; we consume not merely for its own sake—to eat, drink, and enjoy ourselves—but in order to enable more profit-generating production. The reality of this subordinate material position, however, is in regular conflict with enduring popular ideologies proclaiming the power of the so-called sovereign consumer. Consumers, of course, have some freedom, but it is a relative freedom based on the historic establishment and maintenance of a material dependence that presents itself as a natural given of life rather than as an effect of a historically specific political system. What is more, it is a freedom that is contingent, dramatically within a service economy, on the unfreedom of others. That is, the relative freedom we are permitted as consumers helps to suppress the potentially far greater freedom—the freedom to be rather than to buy—that inheres in us as workers and human beings.

Many of us, in the service sector and elsewhere, no doubt bridle at the notion that we "are our jobs" and have often done our best to shrug off the complaints and demands of our traditional bosses. However, it is far more difficult to ignore the ubiquitous and anonymous judgment of a "public" that is amplified on websites read by millions. On the contrary, the combination of our economic dependence on work and the public consumerist surveillance of that work makes it likely that many of us will internalize the latter's logic and values as our own, further enlisting us in our own domination.

NOTES

1. For instance, the Bay Area's Botto Bistro actively encourages customers to write negative, one-star reviews of the restaurant and gives customers stickers that say "I gave Botto one star on Yelp." Botto's owner claims that the restaurant's anti-Yelp campaign—spread via ironic reviews such as "The pizza tastes like the rag at Denny's that they use to wipe down the counters and tabletops"—has improved business (Streitfeld 2016).

2. Joseph Patrick eloquently elaborates similar points in his lecture "Consumption and Consumerism in Capitalism: Myths and Reality," recorded November 9, 2010, in Copenhagen, Denmark.

Bibliography

Adorno, Theodor. 1984 (1967). "Veblen's Attack on Culture." In *Prisms*, 73–94. Cambridge: MIT Press.

Adorno, Theodor, and Max Horkheimer. 2002 (1944). "The Culture Industry." In *Dialectic of Enlightenment*, edited by Theodor Adorno and Max Horkheimer, 94–136. Palo Alto: Stanford University Press.

American Customer Satisfaction Index. 2016a. "ACSI Report on U.S. Economy: The Collapse in Customer Satisfaction Halts." *American Customer Satisfaction Index*. June 29. http://www.theacsi.org/news-and-resources/press-releases/press-2016/press-release-national-acsi-q1-2016.

———. 2016b. "Customer Satisfaction Benchmarks by Sector." *American Customer Satisfaction Index*. http://www.theacsi.org/customer-satisfaction-benchmarks/benchmarks-by-sector

Anderson, Chris. 2006. *The Long Tail: Why the Future of Business Is Selling Less of More*. New York: Hyperion.

———. 2009. *Free: The Future of a Radical Price*. New York: Hyperion.

Andrejevic, Mark. 2004. *Reality TV: The Work of Being Watched*. Lanham, MD: Rowman & Littlefield.

Arrighi, Giovanni. 2006. "Spatial and Other 'Fixes' of Historical Capitalism." In *Global Social Change*, edited by Christopher Chase-Dunn and Salvatore Babones, 201–12. Baltimore: Johns Hopkins University Press.

Arvidsson, A. 2001. "From Counterculture to Consumer Culture: Vespa and the Italian Youth Market, 1958–1978." *Journal of Consumer Culture* 1 (1): 47–71.

———. 2006. *Brands—Meaning and Value in Media Culture*. London: Routledge.

———. 2007. "Creative Class or Administrative Class? On Advertising and the Underground." *Ephemera: Theory & Politics in Organization* 7 (1): 8–23.

Asher-Schapiro, Avi. 2014. "Against Sharing." *Jacobin*, September 19. https://www.jacobinmag.com/2014/09/against-sharing/

Baker, Dean. 2014. "Don't Buy the 'Sharing Economy' Hype: Airbnb and Uber Are Facilitating Rip-Offs." *The Guardian*. May 27. https://www.theguardian.com/commentisfree/2014/may/27/airbnb-uber-taxes-regulation.

Baudrillard, Jean. 2000. "The Ideological Genesis of Needs." In *The Consumer Society Reader*, edited by Juliet Schor and Douglas B. Holt, 57–80. New York: New Press.

———. 1981. *For a Critique of the Political Economy of the Sign*. St. Louis: Telos.

Bauman, Zygmunt. 2004. "The Consumerist Syndrome in Contemporary Society." Interview by Chris Rojek. *Journal of Consumer Culture*, 4 (3): 291–312.

Beller, Jonathan. 2013. "Digitality and the Media of Dispossession." In *Digital Labor*, edited by Trebor Scholz, 165–86. New York: Routledge.

Beniger, James R. 1986. *The Control Revolution: Technological and Economic Origins of the Information Society*. Cambridge, MA: Harvard University Press.
Benkler, Yochai. 2006. *The Wealth of Networks: How Social Production Transforms Markets and Freedom*. New Haven: Yale University Press.
Benson, Susan Porter. 1988. *Counter Cultures*. Chicago: University of Illinois.
Berrett, Dan. 2015. "Can the Student Course Evaluation Be Redeemed?" *Chronicle of Higher Education*, November 29. http://chronicle.com.ezproxy.gc.cuny.edu/article/Can-the-Student-Course/234369.
Bohannon, John. 2016. "Even on eBay, Women Get Paid Less for Their Labor." *Science*. February 19. http://www.sciencemag.org/news/2016/02/even-ebay-women-get-paid-less-their-labor.
Bourdieu, Pierre. 1984. *Distinction*. Cambridge: Harvard University Press.
Bowlby, Rachel. 1987. "Modes of Modern Shopping." In *The Ideology of Conduct*, edited by Nancy Armstrong and Leonard Tennenhouse, 185–205. New York: Methuen.
Brenner, Robert. 2003. *The Boom and the Bubble*. New York: Verso.
Burawoy, Michael. 2009. *The Extended Case Method*. Berkeley: University of California Press.
Burawoy, Michael, ed. 1991. *Ethnography Unbound*. Berkeley: University of California Press.
Chitty, Andrew. 2014. "*Marx and Alienation*, Review by Andrew Chitty." *Marx and Philosophy Society*. http://marxandphilosophy.org.uk/reviewofbooks/reviews/2014/959.
Cohen, Lizabeth. 2003. *A Consumers' Republic: The Politics of Mass Consumption in Postwar America*. New York: Knopf.
Comor, Edward. 2010. "Digital Prosumption and Alienation." *Ephemera* 10 (3/4): 439–54.
Cowan, Ruth Schwartz. 1983. *More Work for Mother: The Ironies of Household Technology from the Open Hearth to the Microwave*. New York: Basic.
Cross, Gary. 1993. "Traumas of Time and Money in Prosperity and Depression." In *Time and Money*, 128–54. London: Routledge.
Cubitt, Sean. 2013. "The Political Economy of Cosmopolis." In *Digital Labor,* edited by Trebor Scholz, 58–68. New York: Routledge.
Davies, Dale. 2014. "Why 'Couchsurfing Is Free' Is a Myth." *Slow Vegan Travel* (blog). http://www.angloitalianfollowus.com/why-couchsurfing-is-free-is-a-myth.
Dean, Jodi. 2013. "Whatever Blogging." In *Digital Labor*, edited by Trebor Scholz, 127–46. New York: Routledge.
De Genova, Nicholas. 2005. *Working the Boundaries*. Durham: Duke University Press.
De Kosnik, Abigail. 2013. "Fandom as Free Labor." In *Digital Labor,* edited by Trebor Scholz, 98–111. New York: Routledge.
DiUlio, Nick. 2010. "Quality Control." *QSR*. June 2010. https://www.qsrmagazine.com/competition/quality-control.
Du Gay, Paul, and Graeme Salaman. 1992. "The [Cult]ure of the Customer." *Journal of Management Studies* 29 (5): 615–33.
Edwards, Richard. 1984. "Forms of Control in the Labor Process." In *Critical Studies in Organization and Bureaucracy*, edited by Frank Fischer and Carmen Sirianni, 86–119. Philadelphia: Temple University Press.
Edelman, Benjamin, and Michael Luca. 2014. "Digital Discrimination: The Case of Airbnb.com." *Harvard Business School Working Paper*, No. 14–54.
Epstein, David. 2006. "'Hotness' and Quality." *Inside Higher Ed*. May 8. https://www.insidehighered.com/news/2006/05/08/rateprof.
Felton, James, Peter T. Koper, John B. Mitchell, and Michael Stinson. 2008. "Attractiveness, Easiness, and Other Issues: Student Evaluations of Professors on RateMyProfessors.com." *Assessment and Evaluation in Higher Education* 33 (1): 45–61.
Fiamengo, Janice. 2013. "How Well Does 'Rate My Professors' Rate?" *PJ Media*. February 23. https://pjmedia.com/blog/how-well-does-rate-my-professors-rate/?singlepage=true.
Fine, Ben, and Ellen Leopold. 1990. "Consumerism and the Industrial Revolution." *Social History* 15 (2): 151–79.
Fiske, John. 2000. "Shopping for Pleasure." In *The Consumer Society Reader*, edited by Juliet Schor and Douglas Holt, 306–28. New York: New Press.

Fisman, Ray, and Michael Luca. 2016. "Fixing Discrimination in Online Marketplaces." *Harvard Business Review*. December. https://hbr.org/2016/12/fixing-discrimination-in-online-marketplaces.

Forbes. 2008. "Methodology." *Forbes.com*. August 13. http://www.forbes.com/2008/08/13/best-colleges-methodology-oped-college08-cx_rv_0813ccap.html.

Foucault, Michel. 2010. *The Birth of Biopolitics: Lectures at the College de France, 1978–1979*. New York: Picador.

———. 1995 [1975]. *Discipline and Punish*. New York: Vintage.

Frank, Thomas, and Matt Weiland, eds. 1997. *Commodify Your Dissent: Salvos from the Baffler*. New York: Norton.

Franklin Benjamin. 2013 [1759]. *Poor Richard's Almanack and Other Writings*. New York: Dover.

Friedman, Milton. 2002 [1962]. *Capitalism and Freedom*. Chicago: University of Chicago Press.

Fuchs, Christian. 2010. "Class, Knowledge and New Media." *Media, Culture and Society* 32 (1): 141–50.

———. 2013. "Social media and capitalism." In *Producing the Internet: Critical Perspectives of Social Media*, edited by Tobias Olsson, 25–44. Göteborg: Nordicom.

———. 2014. "Digital Prosumption Labour on Social Media in the Context of the Capitalist Regime of Time." *Time & Society* 23 (1): 97–123.

Fuller, Linda, and Vicki Smith. 1991. "Consumers' Reports: Management by Customers in a Changing Economy." *Work, Employment, & Society* 5 (1): 1–16.

Gabriel, Yiannis, and Tim Lang. 2015 [1995]. *The Unmanageable Consumer: Contemporary Consumption and Its Fragmentations*. London: Sage Publications.

Galbraith, John. 1958. *The Affluent Society*. Boston: Houghton Mifflin.

Gamble, Jos. 2007. "The Rhetoric of the Consumer and Customer Control in China." *Work, Employment, & Society* 21 (1): 7–25.

Ge, Yanbo, Christopher R. Knittel, Don MacKenzie, and Stephen Zoepf. 2016. "Racial and Gender Discrimination in Transportation Network Companies." *The National Bureau of Economic Research*. NBER Working Paper No. 22776.

Gladwell, Malcolm. 1997. "THE COOLHUNT." *The New Yorker*. March 9. http://www.newyorker.com/magazine/1997/03/17/the-coolhunt.

Glickman, Lawrence B. 1999. *A Living Wage*. Ithaca: Cornell.

———. 2012. *Buying Power*. Chicago: University of Chicago.

Goldberg, Eleanor. 2014. "Vile, Sexist Restaurant Review Prompts Owner to Put Fundraiser on Menu." *Huffpost*, July 28. http://www.huffingtonpost.com/2014/07/28/sexist-restaurant-review-fundraiser_n_5627434.html.

Goodwin, R. Neva, Frank Ackerman, and David Kiron, eds. 1997. *The Consumer Society*. Washington, DC: Island Press.

Graeber, David. 2011. *Debt: The First 5000 Years*. New York: Melville House Publishing.

Griffin, Andrew. 2018. "Snapchat Finally Responds to Petition Criticising New Update after More Than a Million Ask for It to Be Reversed." *The Independent*. February 21. https://www.independent.co.uk/life-style/gadgets-and-tech/news/snapchat-update-new-latest-response-revert-how-to-view-friends-stories-change-a8221661.html.

Hobsbawm, E. J. 1994. *Age of Extremes: The Short Twentieth Century, 1914–1991*. London: Michael Joseph.

Hochschild, Arlie Russell. 2003 [1983]. *The Managed Heart*. Berkeley: University of California.

Holt, Douglas. 2000. "Does Cultural Capital Structure American Consumption." In *The Consumer Society Reader*, edited by Juliet Schor and Douglas Holt, 212–52. New York: New Press.

Hudson, Kris, and Vanessa O'Connell. 2009. "Recession Turns Malls into Ghost Towns." *Wall Street Journal*. May 22. http://www.wsj.com/articles/SB124294047987244803.

Humphrey, Caroline. 1985. "Barter and Economic Disintegration." *Man* 20: 48–72.

Huntsberry, William. 2015. "How We Talk about Our Teachers." *WNYC*. February 23. http://www.wnyc.org/story/how-we-talk-about-our-teachers/.

Illich, Ivan. 1981. *Shadow Work*. Boston: M. Boyars.

Jackson, Kenneth T. 1985. *Crabgrass Frontier: The Suburbanization of the United States*. New York: Oxford University Press.

Jaschik, Scott. 2015. "Accent on Bias." *Inside Higher Ed*, March 2. https://www.insidehighered.com/news/2015/03/02/study-finds-instructors-asian-last-names-receive-lower-scores-rate-my-professors.

Jenkins, Henry. 2006. *Convergence Culture: Where Old and New Media Collide*. New York: New York University Press.

Johnson, Valen. 2003. *Grade Inflation*. New York: Springer.

Judt, Tony. 2005. *Postwar*. New York: Penguin.

Kessler, Sarah. 2015. "The 'Sharing Economy' Is Dead, and We Killed It." *Fast Company*, September 14. https://www.fastcompany.com/3050775/the-sharing-economy-is-dead-and-we-killed-it.

Korczynski, Marek, Karen Shire, Stephen Frenkel, and May Tam. 2000. "Service Work in Consumer Capitalism: Customers, Control and Contradictions." *Work, Employment, & Society* 14 (4): 669–87.

Korczynski, Marek. 2013. "The Customer in the Sociology of Work: Different Ways of Going Beyond the Management-Worker Dyad." *Work, Employment, & Society* 27 (6): NP1–NP7.

Lakshmin, Deepa. 2014. "Here Are the Top 10 Hottest Professors in the Country." *MTV News*. October 24. http://www.mtv.com/news/1974388/rate-my-professors-hottest-ranking/.

Lambert, Craig. 2015. *Shadow Work*. Berkeley: Counterpoint.

Land, Stephanie. 2016. "The Class Politics of Decluttering." *New York Times*. January 18. http://www.nytimes.com/2016/07/18/opinion/the-class-politics-of-decluttering.html?_r=0.

Leidner, Robin. 1993. *Fast Food, Fast Talk*. Berkeley: University of California.

Lewinnek, Elaine. 2014. *The Working Man's Reward*. New York: Oxford University Press.

Lewis, Paul. 2017. "'Our Minds Can Be Hijacked': The Tech Insiders Who Fear a Smartphone Dystopia." *The Guardian*. October 6. https://www.theguardian.com/technology/2017/oct/05/smartphone-addiction-silicon-valley-dystopia.

Lichtenstein, Nelson. 2009. *The Retail Revolution: How Wal-Mart Created a Brave New World of Business*. New York: Metropolitan Books.

Lin, Chien-Huang, and Wen-Hsien Huang. 2006. "The Influence of Unawareness Set and Order Effects in Consumer Regret." *Journal of Business and Psychology* 21 (2): 293–311.

Luca, Michael. 2011. "Reviews, Reputation, and Revenue: The Case of Yelp.com." *Harvard Business School*. Working Paper. September. http://www.hbs.edu/faculty/Publication%20Files/12-016_a7e4a5a2-03f9-490d-b093-8f951238dba2.pdf.

Machanic, Holly. 2015. "How to Respond to Negative Comments on Yelp." *Restaurant Hospitality*. February 9. http://restaurant-hospitality.com/social-media/how-respond-negative-comments-yelp.

Marcuse, Herbert. 1991 [1964]. *One-Dimensional Man*. Boston: Beacon.

Marshall, Aarian. 2017. "As Uber Flails, Its Self-Driving Tech Rolls On." *Wired*, June 23, https://www.wired.com/story/uber-crisis-self-driving-pittsburgh/.

Marx, Karl. 1992 [1867]. *Capital*. Volume 1. London: Penguin.

———. 1993 [1939]. *Grundrisse*. London: Penguin.

———. 1994 [1844]. *Marx: Early Political Writings*, edited by Joseph J. O'Malley and Richard A. Davis. Cambridge: Cambridge University Press.

Maxwell, Joseph. 1992. "Understanding and Validity in Qualitative Research." *Harvard Educational Review* 62 (3): 279–300.

McChesney, Robert. 2013. *Digital Disconnect*. New York: New Press.

McKendrick, Neil. 1982. "The Consumer Revolution of Eighteenth-Century England." In *The Birth of a Consumer Society*, edited by Neil McKendrick, John Brewer, and J. H. Plumb, 9–33. Bloomington: Indiana University Press.

Montell, Gabriela. 2006. "The Art of the Bogus Rating." *The Chronicle of Higher Education*. September 27. http://chronicle.com/article/The-Art-of-the-Bogus-Rating/46887.

Naughton, John. 2014. "Meet Tech's New Concierge Economy, Where Serfs Deliver Stuff to Rich Folk." *The Guardian*, December 27. https://www.theguardian.com/commentisfree/2014/dec/28/uber-amazon-tech-concierge-economy.

Newman, Kathy. 2004. *Radio Active*. Berkeley: University of California Press.
Newton, Casey. 2016. "Facebook May Soon Let Users Collect $$$ on Posts." *CNBC*. April 19. http://www.cnbc.com/2016/04/19/facebook-considers-letting-users-add-a-tip-jar-to-make-money-from-posts.html.
O'Brien, Jeffrey. 2007. "Business Paradigm Shifts and Free Tequila Shots." *Fortune*. July 10. http://archive.fortune.com/magazines/fortune/fortune_archive/2007/07/23/100134489/index.htm.
Otto, James, Douglas A. Sanford, and Douglas N. Ross. 2008. "Does Ratemyprofessor.com Really Rate My Professor?" *Assessment & Evaluation in Higher Education* 33 (4): 355–68.
Patrick, Joseph. 2010. "Consumption and Consumerism in Capitalism: Myths and Reality." Recorded November 2010 in Copenhagen, Denmark. http://ruthlesscriticism.com/Consumption&Consumerism-Copenhagen.mp3.
Paules, Greta. 1991. *Dishing It Out*. Philadelphia: Temple University.
Piketty, Thomas. 2017 [2013]. *Capital in the Twenty-First Century*. Cambridge: Harvard University Press.
Polanyi, Karl. 2001 [1944]. *The Great Transformation*. Boston: Beacon.
Poropat, Arthur. 2014. "Students Don't Know What's Best for Their Own Learning." *The Conversation*. November 18. http://theconversation.com/students-dont-know-whats-best-for-their-own-learning-33835.
Postigo, Hector. 2003. "Emerging Sources of Labor on the Internet: The Case of America Online Volunteers." *International Review of Social History* 48: 205–23.
Powelson, Michael. 2011. "The Proletarianization of the Academy: California State University-Northridge and the California Budget Crisis." *Workplace: A Journal for Academic Labor*. #18.
Prahalad, C. K., and Venkatram Ramaswamy. 2000. "Co-opting Customer Competence." *Harvard Business Review* 78 (January–February): 79–87.
———. 2002. "The Cocreation Connection." *Strategy and Business* 27 (2): 51–60.
———. 2004. "Co-creation Experiences: The Next Practice in Value Creation." *Journal of Interactive Marketing* 18 (3): 5–14.
Presdee, Mike. 1986. "Agony or Ecstasy: Broken Transitions and the New Social State of Working-Class Youth in Australia." South Australian Center for Youth Studies Occasional Paper. Magill, South Australia.
Rafaeli, Anat. 1989. "When Cashiers Meet Customers: An Analysis of the Role of Supermarket Cashiers." *Academy of Management Journal* 32 (2): 245–73.
Rajaee, Shirin. 2017. "Racist Yelp Reviews Left for Restaurant in Downtown Sacramento." *CBS Sacramento*. February 9. http://sacramento.cbslocal.com/2017/02/09/south-restaurant-hit-by-racist-yelp-reviews/.
Ramaswamy, Chitra. 2017. "'Prejudices Play Out in the Ratings We Give'—The Myth of Digital Equality." *The Guardian*. February 20. https://www.theguardian.com/technology/2017/feb/20/airbnb-uber-sharing-apps-digital-equality.
Rate My Professors. 2015. "About Rate My Professors.com." Viacom International.
———. 2018. "About Rate My Professors.com." *Viacom International*. July 27. http://www.ratemyprofessors.com/About.jsp.
Rey, P. J. 2012. "Alienation, Exploitation, and Social Media." *American Behavioral Scientist* 56 (4): 399–420.
Ritzer, George. 2004. *The McDonaldization of Society*. Thousand Oaks, CA: Pine Forge Press.
———. 2010. *Enchanting a Disenchanted World: Revolutionizing the Means of Consumption*. Thousand Oaks: Pine Forge.
Ritzer, George, and Nathan Jurgenson. 2010. "Production, Consumption, Prosumption: The Nature of Capitalism in the Age of the Digital 'Prosumer.'" *Journal of Consumer Culture* 10 (1): 13–36.
Ritzer, George, Paul Dean, and Nathan Jurgenson. 2012. "The Coming of Age of the Prosumer." *American Behavioral Scientist* 56 (4): 379–98.
Roediger, David. 2007 [1991]. *The Wages of Whiteness*. New York: Verso.

Roose, Kevin. 2014. "The Sharing Economy Isn't about Trust, It's about Desperation." *New York*. April 24. http://nymag.com/daily/intelligencer/2014/04/sharing-economy-is-about-desperation.html.

Ross, Andrew. 2013. "In Search of the Lost Paycheck." In *Digital Labor,* edited by Trebor Scholz, 13–32. New York: Routledge.

Schmidt, Ben. 2015. "Gendered Language in Teacher Reviews." *Gendered Language in Teaching Evaluations*. February.

Scholz, Trebor. 2013. "Introduction." In *Digital Labor,* edited by Trebor Scholz, 1–10. New York: Routledge.

Schor, Juliet. 1998. *The Overspent American*. New York: Harper.

———. 2014. "Debating the Sharing Economy." Great Transition Initiative. October.

Schor, Juliet, and Douglas B. Holt, eds. 2000. *The Consumer Society Reader*. New York: New Press.

Sherman, Rachel. 2007. *Class Acts: Service and Inequality in Luxury Hotels*. Berkeley: University of California Press.

Simmel, Georg. 1957 [1904]. "Fashion." *American Journal of Sociology* 62 (6): 541–58.

Srnicek, Nick. 2017. *Platform Capitalism*. Cambridge, UK: Polity Press.

Slee, Tom. 2013. "Some Obvious Things about Internet Reputation Systems." *Tom Slee* (blog). September 29. http://tomslee.net/2013/09/some-obvious-things-about-internet-reputation-systems.html.

———. 2014. "Sharing and Caring." *Jacobin*. January 24. https://www.jacobinmag.com/2014/01/sharing-and-caring.

———. 2016. "The Sharing Economy's Dirty Laundry." *Jacobin*. March 23. https://www.jacobinmag.com/2016/03/uber-airbnb-sharing-economy-housing-tech.

Smith, Adam. 2003 [1776]. *The Wealth of Nations*. New York: Bantam.

Sperber, Joshua. 2014. "Yelp and Labor Discipline." *New Labor Forum* 23 (2): 68–74.

———. 2018. "Making the Grade." *New Labor Forum* 27 (1): 36–43.

Steylaerts, Vicky, and Sean O'Dubhghaill. 2012. "CouchSurfing and Authenticity: Notes Towards an Understanding of an Emerging Phenomenon." *Hospitality and Society* 1 (3): 261–78.

Streitfeld, David. 2016. "Online Reviews? Researchers Give Them a Low Rating." *New York Times*. June 7. http://www.nytimes.com/2016/06/09/technology/online-reviews-researchers-give-them-a-low-rating.html?_r=0.

Stroebe, Wolfgang. 2016. "Why Good Teaching Evaluations May Reward Bad Teaching." *Perspectives on Psychological Science* 11 (6): 800–16.

Subtirelu, Nicholas. 2015. "'She Does Have an Accent but . . .': Race and Language Ideology in Students' Evaluations of Mathematics Instructors on RateMyProfessors.com." *Language in Society* 44 (1): 35–62.

Sundararajan, Arun. 2016. *The Sharing Economy*. Cambridge: MIT.

Swidler, Eva. 2018. Comment on "Making the Grade: Rating Professors." *New Labor Forum*. January.

Tapscott D., and A. Williams. 2006. *Wikinomics: How Mass Collaboration Changes Everything*. New York: Penguin.

Terranova, Tiziana. 2000. "Free Labor: Producing Culture for Digital Economy." *Social Text* 18 (2): 33–58.

Toffler, Alvin. 1980. *The Third Wave*. New York: Bantam Books.

Tolich, Martin B. 1993. "Alienating and Liberating Emotions at Work: Supermarket Clerks' Performance of Customer Service." *Journal of Contemporary Ethnography* 22 (3): 361–81.

Twenge, Jean. 2017. "Have Smartphones Destroyed a Generation?" *The Atlantic*. September. https://www.theatlantic.com/magazine/archive/2017/09/has-the-smartphone-destroyed-a-generation/534198/.

Veblen, Thorstein. 1994 [1899]. *The Theory of the Leisure Class*. New York: Macmillan.

Virilio, Paul. 2012. *The Administration of Fear*. Los Angeles: Semiotext.

Ward, Jane. 2008. "Dude Sex." *Sexuality* 11 (4): 414–34.

Warner, Lloyd, Marsha Meeker, and Kenneth Eells. 1949. *Social Class in America*. New York: Harper Torchbooks.

Watkins, Evan. 1993. *Throwaways: Work Culture and Consumer Education*. Stanford, CA: Stanford University Press.

Weber, Max. 2002 [1905]. *The Protestant Ethic and the Spirit of Capitalism*. New York: Penguin.

White, Martha C. 2012. "Does Not Having a Facebook Page Make You 'Suspicious' to Employers?" *Time*. August 8. http://business.time.com/2012/08/08/does-not-having-a-facebook-page-make-you-suspicious-to-employers/.

Williamson, Judith. 1986. *Decoding Advertisements*. London: Marion Boyars.

Wu, Tim. 2014. "Why Airlines Want to Make You Suffer." *The New Yorker*. December 26. http://www.newyorker.com/business/currency/airlines-want-you-to-suffer.

Yaraghi, Niam, and Shamika Ravi. 2017. "The Current and Future State of the Sharing Economy." *Brookings India* IMPACT Series No. 032017.

Yelp. 2018. "About Us." *Yelp.com*. http://www.yelp.com/about.

Zervas, Georgios, Davide Proserpio, and John Byers. 2015. "A First Look at Online Reputation on Airbnb, Where Every Stay Is above Average." January 28. https://papers.ssrn.com/sol3/papers.cfm?abstract_id=2554500.

Zimmerman, Jonathan. 2014. "The Real Scandal Behind the Yale Course Website." *Washington Post*. January 24. https://www.washingtonpost.com/opinions/the-real-scandal-behind-the-yale-course-web-site/2014/01/24/f719ef56-8449-11e3-9dd4-e7278db80d86_story.html?utm_term=.c6d387f79989.

Žižek, Slavoj. 2009. *The Sublime Object of Ideology*. New York: Verso.

Zukin, Sharon, Scarlett Lindeman, and Laurie Hurson. 2015. "The Omnivore's Neighborhood? Online Restaurant Reviews, Race, and Gentrification." *Journal of Consumer Culture*, 17 (3): 459–79.

Zwick, D., S. K. Bonsu, and A. Darmody. 2008. "Putting Consumers to Work: 'Co-creation' and New Marketing Govern-mentality." *Journal of Consumer Culture* 8 (2): 163–96.

Index

About the Author

A native of Los Angeles, **Joshua Sperber** lives in southern Virginia where he is assistant professor of political science and history at Averett University. His writings have appeared in *New Labor Forum*, *Z Magazine*, *The Journal of Palestine Studies*, and *Counterpunch.*

www.ingramcontent.com/pod-product-compliance
Ingram Content Group UK Ltd.
Pitfield, Milton Keynes, MK11 3LW, UK
UKHW012042150926
475560UK00001B/146

9 781498 592215